READY, STUDY, GO.

Khurshed holds an M.Sc. in mathematics from IIT Bombay. He is a Parsi and is fondly called Bawa, a nickname he inherited from his IIT days. More than twenty years ago, he decided he would rather teach people how to meditate and make them happy instead of teaching them mathematics and making them miserable. He became an Art of Living teacher and this allowed him to do exactly that, and gave him the freedom to explore many of his varied passions.

He loves music and plays the piano, is a foodie and runs the Cafe at the Art of Living Bangalore Ashram. He has created workshops to teach mind mapping, mathematics, cooking yummy vegetarian food and how to understand and appreciate western classical music.

Dinesh holds a B.Tech. in metallurgy and material science from IIT Bombay. He always wanted to make a difference to the people around him and the world in general. At the age of twenty he became an Art of Living teacher and has taught in more than thirty countries.

He is a fitness enthusiast and thoroughly enjoys his daily workouts. He is a sportsman and loves to play soccer. He has a unique and at times humorous take on current affairs, which he prolifically expresses through his tweets.

Bawa and **Dinesh** have taught people from all sections of society – from corporate courses to courses in slums, from terrorists in jails to fresh budding minds in the premier educational institutions of the country.

They have run several innovative social projects for the Art of Living. Notable among them are Donate a Book, Educate a Child, The Great Green Project in which about a 1,00,000 trees were planted, The March against Corruption and The Mumbai Hopeline to help prevent suicides.

Under the guidance of Sri Sri Ravi Shankar, they designed Art of Living's flagship youth program YES!+ (Youth Empowerment and Skills), which is offered in more than 100 countries worldwide.

Bawa and Dinesh have a YouTube channel www.youtube.com/bndtv that has videos on spirituality, mathematics, fitness and many of their other interests. Some of their videos are viral, with more than a few lakh views. You will find more posts and details on their website www.bawandinesh.in.

They live in a beautiful home surrounded by nature in the Art of Living Bangalore Ashram with their friends, who are their family, all of whom contributed in some way or the other to this book.

Facebook: www.facebook.com/khurshedbatliwala and
www.facebook.com/dineshghodke

Twitter: www.twitter.com/khurshed and
www.twitter.com/dineshghodke

Advanced Praise for *Ready, Study, Go!*

'I thoroughly enjoyed reading *Ready, Study, Go!* There is immense positive energy as the book unfolds page after page. It explores the multiple connectivities that are there within us and helps us understand how we can learn effectively and efficiently, and possibly even live better.

As I read the book many questions surfaced and the answers emerged as if the authors were listening to my questions and answering them. The illustrations are cheerful and bring clarity to the matter. It is a fantastic, unputdownable book, and I would heartily recommend it to be read by absolutely everyone!'

—**Dr Indira Parikh**, former dean ANTARDISHA, founder president FLAME University, former dean IIM Ahmedabad

'An innovative, fun and healthy approach to learning, loving learning and loving what you learn!'

—**Emma Seppälä, PhD**, science director, Center for Compassion and Altruism Research and Education, Stanford University School of Medicine

'This book inspires me to want to keep studying.

If applied in student life, the techniques described will not only help you become a better learner but automatically help you imbibe the self-discipline and concentration that is required to succeed. Brilliant read not just for students but for anyone who wants to learn!'

—**Pratik Poddar**, All India Rank 3, IITJEE 2006, All India Rank 2, AIEEE 2006, B.Tech. Computer Science, IIT-B

'How did you prepare for JEE? How many hours did you study? Can you give me some tips on how to go about JEE preparation? These are some of the questions I have been asked multiple times.

Big thanks to Bawa and Dinesh for *Ready, Study, Go!* This wonderful book answers all these questions and much more in simple, yet profound and amazingly fun ways.'

—**Achin Bansal**, All India Rank 1, IITJEE 2007,
B.Tech. Computer Science, IIT-B

'*Ready, Study, Go!* is an Alice in Wonderland tour of fascinating facts and tips on how to get the most out of your studies.

This is one of the most fun and handy books we have ever read. It's a complete DIY book on how to prepare for exams, for important meetings, in fact for any sort of learning you may need to do. It's about learning to learn.

And the wonderful thing is that it will appeal to anyone between the ages of 14 to 87. It's a must read. A definite book to buy and keep by your side.'

—**Prama and Ranji Bhandari**, patron and founders,
Harvard Club of India

'Writing in very lucid style, Bawa and Dinesh address the root cause of challenges a student faces while studying and give pragmatic tips to address them. Their practical experience of working with thousands of students worldwide shines through in this riveting book.'

—**Muralidhar Koteshwar**, B.Tech., IIT-M, visiting professor
IIT-B, managing director, Sonim

'A very relatable and readable book for students of all ages by two achievers I know well! Bawa and Dinesh break down mastering the art of studying, and show how achieving the grades one has always dreamed of can become a reality. I would recommend this book to my nieces and all students at all levels, and am personally empowered to be armed with it at the start of my own daughter's academic life!'

—**Lara Dutta Bhupathi**, mom, actress and
Miss Universe 2000

'My love for studies came back after reading *Ready, Study, Go!* The brain hacks covered in the book have helped me to learn at a much faster speed as compared to earlier. I am able to study effectively for longer stretches, sometimes exceeding 5-6 hours. The technique of Mind mapping I learned from the book has become an indispensable part of my work.'

—**Nitin Agarwal**, undergraduate Computer Science,
IIT Delhi, All India Rank 156, 2011

'It has given me a user manual for the best hardware of my body!'

—**Rohan Kumar Gayari**, M.Tech. Mathematics and
Computing, IIT Delhi

'The How to Study chapter in the book has boosted my productivity to amazing levels. Enjoyed the book.'

—**Vaibhav Sharma**, undergraduate Electrical,
IIT Delhi, All India Rank 234

'I truly understand the process of learning now. A true eye opener that empowered me with practical solutions and understandings of my mind.'

—**Parth Shah**, undergraduate, IIT Delhi,
All India Rank 91

'I thoroughly enjoyed reading the book. It was a nice experience. Study nowadays has become so complicated that students are being pressurised and having unnecessary burden. This book gives you an insight about how studying can be easy. The techniques mentioned are quite simple yet profound. The charts and brain maps shape the child's way of learning into a interesting mode rather than cramming up things. I would suggest every student looking for efficient and smart ways of learning to give it a read.'

—**Parth Sharma**, AIR 2, AIIMS entrance exam

'To limit this book to just "Study" is really misleading

It is about 'Using your Brain' and using it well – something that almost anyone would want to learn. An invaluable tool on how the brain ticks, what keeps it going fast and what slows it down.

A must for professionals – at some point, we all hit a plateau in our thinking – we get stuck in repetitive thinking and doing styles.

This book will help you pole-vault those plateaus.

Compelling content, memorable writing style. Read it and make sure people around you read it too.'

—**Pratibha Iyer**, CEO, Pratima Arts

'I have the good fortune of doing an Art of Living course with Dinesh circa 2001. Through Dinesh I got introduced to Bawa, perhaps the wittiest personality at Art of Living.

This book touches upon absolutely every aspect concerning studying today. It's a recipe of enriching facts, effective techniques and quite a few dashes of great humour, combined with the secret sauce of experience dished out with panache by Dinesh and Bawa.

Please write more ... Waiting to see what you come up with next!'

—**VSS Mani**, CEO, Just Dial

'This book provides awesome practical tips to keep the mind fresh and focused. It helps bring about a change in the way one approaches studying. The methodologies discussed in the book have the potential of making the process of learning enjoyable and interesting.'

—**Pentala Harikrishna**, Chess Grandmaster,
Arjuna Awardee, World Junior Champion,
Common Wealth Champion, Asian Champion,
Current World Rank 12

'One thing that I did not appreciate about this book is the fact that it was released only after I had finished my regular academics. I realised how much more I could have achieved by studying more effectively. This book is really a treasure if students want to plan meticulously, think rationally and act decisively in working towards their curriculum. Written in a frank, conversational style, that is the hallmark of Bawa and Dinesh, this book is definitely mandatory reading, not only for youngsters still studying but also for all of us who are students of life. Chapters on meditation, surya namaskars, exercise and on mind maps would keep reminding me in the future on how to plan diligently and accomplish more in the future.

A big thank you for coming up with this long overdue book.'

—**Raghoo Puri**, IFS (Indian Foreign
Service Officer)

'Flipping through the book that you are holding right now my initial reaction was "Wow! Such a lovely book, I wish I had the opportunity to read such book while I was giving exams in my school/college life." However, after reading more and more pages at some point I felt like "Wait a minute, this is useful for everyone! This is beneficial for me right now."

I had the opportunity to spend some quality time with both authors and learned a lot of things. I always loved the simplicity in their way of explaining intricate things of life hence it's not a surprise for me to see the way authors explained many intriguing details with crystal clear explanations in this book. The simplicity of the book makes the reading journey very enjoyable.

There are chapters on health and food habits, developing the subconscious mind and intuition, party tips(!), exercise, even some simple delicious recipes. There is a lot covered in this book, all dished out with a generous sprinkling of laughter.

Get the book, read it, and you will be *Ready, Study, Go!*'
—**Surya Shekar Ganguly**, Chess Grandmaster, Arjuna Awardee, Asian Champion and six times National Champion

'It is said that learning should be a joyous activity. It enriches one with new knowledge and ways of being and succeeding in the world. "Vidya Sarvatra Bhushanam" goes the Sanskrit proverb. Since time immemorial, education has always been seen as the true wealth which one carries everywhere.

In today's hyper-competitive world, formal education systems tend to focus on learning through rote and memory and often fail at developing the student's true potential. I have seen many students who graduate with formal degrees, have performed well in academics, but lack analytical and practical life skills and are unable to deal with problems and failures effectively.

Ready, Study, Go! brings a fresh perspective on learning, the purpose of education and answers very poignant questions being posed by students and educators everywhere. An immensely readable book, the authors share insights from their decades-long experience of working with students. Khurshed and Dinesh have very beautifully woven together insights on all the aspects of an individual that require nourishment during student life.

I highly recommend this book for all students and parents who are seeking to change the paradigm of learning and make it a truly enjoyable activity.'

—**Dr Ajay Tejasvi Narasimhan**, Program Manager,
Collaborative Leadership for Development Program,
Equitable Growth, Finance and Institutions Vice-Presidency,
The World Bank Group, Washington D.C.

'I would highly recommend *Ready, Study, Go!*, no matter what stage they are in life. We are human beings, and we are always learning. I for one, love learning new stuff. I hold a few degrees now – in acting, medicine, fashion entrepreneurship and film directing, and this book covers everything I could wish it to have, to be able to with much less effort, learn any of those things.

So far, I had never come across a really good book detailing the process of learning. This one is exactly that. It has so much content, all of it presented in such a crisp, articulate and enjoyable style. Not only does it teach you how to study any subject; it has tips and techniques to enhance your general health and lifestyle.

It creates clarity in your mind, leading to more productive and efficient ways of getting your work done.'

—**Fagun Thakrar**, fashion designer, actor-writer-director, Hollywood

'A long time ago, Swami Vivekananda had rightly pointed out the unlimited capability of the human brain. This book will be of great help for students to prepare for various competitive examinations in a smart way by utilising the brain's hidden potential.'

—**Nishant Jain**, IAS, 2015 Batch, Rank 13, UPSC CSE-2014

'Transcending from current day practice of rote learning to acquiring pearls of wisdom through a deeper understanding of the subject is the need of the hour and this book helps in instilling this confidence while making learning fun.

Kudos to authors for sharing their nectar of experience while working with thousands of student across the spectrum over many years. I would urge all students, teachers and parents to have this as a must read.'

—**Satya Bansal**, CEO, Barclays Wealth

'The book breaks the general conception of studying being an isolated activity and explains how it has so many facets and connections with all other aspects of life. It changes the whole idea of studying from being mundane, boring and dreadful to being exciting, fun and almost sacred. A must read for students, professionals, businesspeople and anyone who has had a complicated relationship with studies.'

—**Divyam Gupta**, Chartered Accountant

READY, STUDY, GO!

Smart Ways to Learn

KHURSHED BATLIWALA
AND DINESH GHODKE

———————Illustrated by———————

*Dr Deepa Chettiar, Susha, Rupal, Zubin and
Gowrishankar*

HarperCollins *Publishers* India

First published in India in 2016 by
HarperCollins *Publishers* India

Copyright © Khurshed Batliwala and Dinesh Ghodke 2016

P-ISBN: 978-93-5264-134-5
E-ISBN: 978-93-5264-135-2

4 6 8 10 9 7 5

Khurshed Batliwala and Dinesh Ghodke assert the moral right
to be identified as the authors of this work.

The views and opinions expressed in this book
are the authors' own and the facts are as reported by them,
and the publishers are not in any way liable for the same.

HarperCollins *Publishers*
A-75, Sector 57, Noida, Uttar Pradesh 201301, India
1 London Bridge Street, London SE1 9GF, United Kingdom
Hazelton Lanes, 55 Avenue Road, Suite 2900, Toronto, Ontario M5R 3L2
and 1995 Markham Road, Scarborough, Ontario M1B 5M8, Canada
25 Ryde Road, Pymble, Sydney, NSW 2073, Australia
195 Broadway, New York, NY 10007, USA

Typeset in 11/14.6 Adobe Garamond at
Manipal Digital Systems, Manipal

Printed and bound at
Thomson Press (India) Ltd.

CONTENTS

PREFACE (BAWA)

The first time I failed came as an absolute shock to me.

Not seeing your roll number on the list of graduating students is a truly terrible feeling. There are people whooping with joy all around you, and all you feel is that terrible sinking sensation in your stomach and a constricting heaviness in your chest as you begin to accept the horrific reality of failure and how you are going to face the world from then on.

I had been a fairly good student throughout my life, scoring in the upper sixties at the very least, sometimes even hitting the nineties. This time, however, I had not prepared enough. These were my final year exams for a bachelors' degree in mathematics and I had relied on clearing one of the papers by copying from a friend. It didn't quite work out, and I lost a year by seven marks.

It was quite a jolt, and after I finished punishing myself – no music, no friends, no TV, no computer games, etc., for about a month – I pulled myself together and decided to really study.

The next time I gave the exam, in October, I missed first class by seven marks. To prove a point to myself, I retook the exam the following year in May, this time becoming the college topper. I also helped two friends clear the exam, one who had failed five consecutive attempts and the other who was giving it for the first time. Both got first class.

After that, I dabbled around for a bit until a good friend of mine took me to meet his buddy, who was studying at IIT Bombay. Until that point, I had never ever even considered applying to IIT because I had thought that studying there required a very different mental make-up from the one I had.

When I did meet a few people studying at IIT, I found them to be normal (or very near it)… I suddenly found myself thinking that if those guys could manage to get to the hallowed halls of India's most prestigious technical institution, I should be able to do it too!

It was too late for me to give the JEE and do a B.Tech., but a master's degree seemed well within my reach.

The entrance exam was such that absolutely anything could be asked. Right from school to B.Sc. levels – and so I set about mastering my subject with determination. I had just a few weeks to accomplish the task, but managed pretty well, ranking fifteen in a group of more than 2,000 people who took the entrance exam.

My troubles began after the first few lectures I attended. It turned out that IIT was not much different from any other educational institution. You were supposed to make notes of what the professor wrote on the board and vomit it on to the answer sheet during exam time. Accurate vomiting got better grades.

It was not all bad, however. There were glimmers of wonder in the otherwise pedestrian teaching at IIT-B and some brilliant teachers rekindled the love for learning that the others systematically tried to extinguish.

To be able to get good grades in almost every subject notwithstanding the brilliance (or lack of) of the teacher teaching it was a formidable challenge. I managed to flunk yet again, but by the time I finished my master's degree, I had a few professors encouraging me to do a PhD with them and a few others saying that I should go to the US and that they would give me glowing recommendations for the same.

I had also through bitter experience learnt how to learn. I had learnt the art of studying.

This book contains my secrets.

All the very best!

Jai Gurudeva!

Bawa

PREFACE (DINESH)

I loved school. Every single year I would get the award in school for not missing a single day. I used to enjoy learning. Learning new things gave me kicks even before I experienced alcohol or meditation.

In Grade 12, I missed getting into IIT where my elder brother was already studying. I dropped a year, didn't take admission anywhere and studied exclusively for the IIT JEE. It made family members and sundry relatives extremely unhappy and nervous at the idea of losing a year, but I stuck to my decision. IIT JEE was one of the toughest exams in the world where more than 3,00,000 students appeared and just around 3,000 were selected. The coming year I managed to get through by sheer hard work.

IIT hit me hard. I had always been in the top ten of my class and in IIT I was somewhere near the bottom. I got pitted against the best of the best. I did manage to get in, but I got the extremely unglamorous metallurgy and material science specialization. I challenge anyone to find a more boring thing to study.

I took keen interest in sports and extracurricular activities. I volunteered with the Art of Living Foundation. I remained an average student and managed to get through and graduated. Amazingly though, I landed the most coveted job through our campus placements which was paying me more monthly than what my dad earned in a year and way ahead of my batch mates or my brother who had done MS and started working in the US. I could ascribe that to the life skills I learnt from being mentored by Bawa and volunteering for Art of Living.

I didn't take that job, as it would mean I would have to leave India and I was too much in love with my country to consider that. I really wanted to contribute to India and first make a difference to the people around me.

I worked with Infosys for a little more than a year before I became a full-time faculty with the Art of Living.

From dropping a year to getting the best job on campus to becoming Art of Living's youngest teacher was quite a journey. More than a decade later, Bawa and I, under the guidance of Sri Sri Ravi Shankar, created the YES!* course – Youth Empowerment and Skills – for young people above the age of eighteen. It is Art of Living's flagship programme for youth and is offered in more than 100 countries worldwide.

We used to have one constant question from students almost everywhere. How do I concentrate on my studies?!

I must confess, I didn't have the answer to that, but Bawa did. He agreed to write a book about it but only if I helped. Though we started with the idea of answering just that one question, we quickly realized, through our own experiences and discussions, that effective studying could never be an isolated activity. There was so much that surrounded it – fitness, the ability to work in groups, handling relationships, dealing with failure, leading teams … the list is long.

The result was this book.

You are holding in your hands the distilled knowledge of what we learnt through our victories and our failures over the last twenty-five years.

We had a fabulous time. Now it's your turn.

Ready, Study, GO!

Jai Gurudeva!

Dinesh

ACKNOWLEDGEMENTS

It was a blessed day when I stumbled into Art of Living and had the immense fortune of being with my beloved Gurudev, Sri Sri Ravi Shankar. This book and most of the charmed life I lead comes from His Grace.

Dinesh is my co-conspirator in almost everything I do. He has the patience of a few saints and the solidity of a mountain range. He walked into my class so many years ago and thankfully never left. Life is fantastic because of him.

Gowrishankar and Abhiram, for bringing to the screen in such vivid and wonderful ways so many ideas in our heads that would otherwise have had to stay there. And for all the countless things they do around us so that things work and life is simpler and so much more fun.

Mom and Dad. All moms and dads are special, but mine are super special! Their support and encouragement, their belief in my dreams and most importantly, their love makes me what I am today.

My sister Perviz, her husband Carl and their kids Aarman, Ahun and Bhuvana for teaching me about love and patience.

Francois and Namrita, for their belief that we could actually write and recommending our work to HarperCollins.

Salman, for helping create our online presence.

Mayur, for the milk!

Prama and Ranji Bhandari, for sharing their exquisite home with us. For all the wonderful food and sparkling conversation.

Shavina, for taking care of us and pampering us at every opportunity she gets.

Dhruv Kaura, for gifting us his laptop when all our machines had crashed. The show went on because of his spontaneous generosity.

Abhay Joshi, for all the little things and big things.

Lalit, for posing and shaving.

Rosy, for making things easy and super comfortable for us – on the ground and up in the air!

Harish, Avinash, Mahika and Rashmin for their contributions to this book.

Dr Deepa Chettiar, Rupal, Susha, Zubin and Bharati for their lovely illustrations and for infusing beauty into this book.

Dr Ankita Dhelia, Dr Surya Ramesh and Dr Pinkita for all their inputs and research.

Anjana, for saying she would be the first one to buy my book!

Debasri, from HarperCollins, for saying yes!

Chaital, Milan and their families, for all the good times.

All my chefs at Café Vishala – Kamesh, PD, Kuldeep, Prasad and the others for providing nourishment at all times of the day and night.

Gratitude for all who read various bits and pieces of this book and helped make it better.

Humongous thanks to you, dear reader, for buying this book and deciding to read it. There is quite an adventure awaiting you...

Jai Gurudeva!
Love,

Bawa 'n' Dinesh

THE SEVEN LEVELS

We exist on seven levels. These are the Body, Breath, Mind, Memory, Intellect, Ego and Self.

We usually club the mind, memory and intellect into one unit and call it the 'mind'. For many people, 'studying' seems to be a function of just this 'mind' (the mind-memory-intellect combo). They are quite wrong. Effective studying happens only when all seven levels of our existence are being nourished properly. Just as a good building is not simply the roof, floors and walls – but is a fantastic combination of those and many other elements such as the slope of the land, the climate, and the materials being used – truly effective studying happens only when all seven levels are taken care of.

The body is the gross aspect of a living being. If you don't have a body, chances are you will not need textbooks or any other tip or tool described in this book to study. The body needs to be well taken care of. Proper exercise, yoga and a good diet will contribute big time towards great grades. An unhealthy body can greatly hamper your ability to study and perform well.

We all breathe. The breath is the only physiological function of the body over which we have some level of control. We can breathe faster or slower. We can hold the breath for a bit. Every emotion that we experience triggers a breathing pattern and conversely, a particular breathing pattern will usually trigger an emotion. Positive emotions are typically associated with long deep breaths and negative emotions trigger short, shallow, sharp breaths. Some sort of control over the breathing helps maintain a sense of calmness in adverse situations, allowing us to take good decisions. This is the essence of the science of Pranayama.

The mind is what we use to experience the universe around us, through the five senses. At any moment, there is a tremendous amount of stimulus being received by our senses. If we were aware of every last bit of it – if everything around us could impact us – then we would go crazy in a few seconds. The mind filters out stuff that is irrelevant and extraneous, making us experience only the things that are important.

Have you ever worn a watch after a long time of not wearing anything on your wrist? Did you notice how when you first wore it, you kept feeling it there, but in a few days you barely notice it? That's the mind kicking in. To begin with it feels the watch as alien and something new, so it gives you the experience of wearing it. Later, once it has 'accepted' the watch as something that is constantly there, it makes you become almost unaware of it.

The mind is incredibly powerful at manifesting things you want. But it is also very innocent and cannot differentiate between a desire and a fear or an aversion. Have you noticed how when you don't like someone and you don't want to see them, they keep 'coincidentally' meeting you or getting in touch with you? This is your mind at work.

Making an intention clear is a delicate art. For example, instead of saying 'I shouldn't fail', you should say 'I should get great grades!' The mind will latch on to the most powerful words – 'fail' or 'great' in this instance – and manifest that for you. It will actually create situations around you that will make this happen. For the same reason, you should not have many intentions at the same time. This confuses the mind and nothing or very little happens. When you can get the mind to work for you, you become almost unstoppable.

The intellect is your decision-making faculty. The intellect judges and discriminates. The memory stores past experiences. The intellect looks into the memory and then judges whether a particular thing should or shouldn't be done.

For example: you are near an ice cream shop. The intellect goes into the memory and sees that the last time you ate ice cream it felt wonderful. So it says, 'Go on, eat it, eat it!'

Say you are near fire on a cold day. The intellect goes in the memory and sees that some time ago you had been burned by a fire, which caused you pain; at the same time, it also remembers how nice and cosy you felt near a fire when it was cold. So it says to you, 'It's OK to be close to fire for the heat, but don't go too close; be careful.'

The intellect also doubts. When there is stress, the intellect goes into 'doubt mode' and all good judgements go for a toss. Doubt can severely hamper your studying ability and your chances of success in the world. There are three types of doubts.

stress = Doubt !

Doubts about yourself and your abilities – I am not good enough; I don't think I can do this; I am hopeless; I cannot make any friends; I am pathetic at relationships, etc.

Doubts about the world in general – everyone is out to get me; I am not safe; no one likes me or loves me, etc.

Doubt in what you are doing – there is no point in studying this; this cannot possibly help me in the future, etc.

These are life-debilitating thoughts and can very quickly turn a happy, successful person into a nervous wreck.

Because of stress, the memory can get into the bad habit of clinging on to negative experiences you have had and then 'eternalizing' them. For example, getting stuck in a rut over past mistakes or failures, instead of drawing inspiration and hope from past achievements. Statements like 'I always fall sick during exams', 'No one loves me or cares for me' are examples of this. Be careful of releasing those intentions into the universe; the mind will manifest them for you.

The ego is that sense of 'I' that you have. A healthy ego is inclusive and loves to succeed along with others. It also learns from failure and mistakes and makes you genuinely concerned when others fail. It makes you feel big and generous. A healthy ego likes to give credit to others when credit is due and takes responsibility when things are going wrong. It puts a glow on your face and makes you smile more.

A sick ego is exclusive, born out of fear and feels jealous of others' successes. Instead of learning from mistakes, it blames people and situations. It feels glee when others fail. A sick ego makes you feel small and stingy. A sick ego will refuse to take responsibility for failure and will almost never give any credit to others who contributed to your success. A sick ego makes you feel old and tired, and you hardly smile.

It is of critical importance for the mind to be calm, for the intellect to be doubt-free, for the memory to be clear and for the ego to be healthy. Then, one can perceive reality clearly and take rational, intelligent decisions. Only through awareness of yourself and the various building blocks that make 'you' can you truly succeed. The easiest way to bring about this awareness is by learning and regularly practising meditation.

The Self cannot be defined. It's your very core. A glimpse of who you truly are can happen when you meditate. This brings great energy and stamina and you can achieve stuff you never ever dreamed possible.

When the seven levels are healthy and synchronized, then success comes almost effortlessly. Good luck follows you.

THE
SUPERCALIFRAGILISTICEXPIALIDOCIOUS
BODY

The odds of you being you are so remote that it's an absolute miracle that you are indeed you.

One calculation puts the odd at 1 to $10^{2685000}$.

That's a big number. It's far bigger than the number of particles in the universe. In fact, it's much bigger than the number of particles that would be in the universe if the universe itself were made up of particles, each of which was a universe!

Think about it. First of all, your parents had to have met and liked each other enough to get intimate. They would have needed to have sex at the exact moment they did. If your mom told your dad, 'Not tonight, darling, I have a headache'. Poof! You vanish. And it goes further than that; since you are made up of the genetic information from your dad and mom, their parents would have needed to have met and have had sex when they did for your parents to be even born ... and so on until the beginning of time. 'You' are an adventure four and a half billion years in the making!

Out of around 250 million sperm, you are made of that one sperm that managed to reach the egg deep inside the fallopian tubes and fertilize it first. You started life by being the champion in the only race that really matters, the most important race you would ever run (or swim). You (and me), all of us, started as winners!

The prize for winning that race is called Life.

We live our life in this vehicle called the body. The body is made of stuff that would put any science fiction or fantasy you could care to name to shame.

Your nose can remember 50,000 different scents.

More than 1,00,000 chemical reactions take place in your brain every second.

An average human being is made up of seven billion, billion, billion atoms. There is a lot of you!

You have more than 1,50,000 km of arteries, veins and capillaries inside you.

Human bones are as strong as granite. A one-inch block of human bone can hold nine tons of weight.

The human eye can distinguish ten million different colours. If it were a digital camera, the resolution would be around 576 megapixels.

If a baby continued to grow at the rate it was growing around the fourth and fifth week of a pregnancy, the birth-weight would be in excess of ten tons.

Our heartbeats change and mimic the music we are listening to.

There are more bacteria in your mouth than there are people on the planet.

In each cell of our body is a nucleus. In each microscopic nucleus are strands of DNA containing the genetic blueprint of your life. If a strand of DNA from just one nucleus of just one cell were stretched out, it would be six feet long.

Your brain's long-term memory will hold one quadrillion bits of information in your lifetime.

When you take one step, you use around 200 muscles.

If the acid in your stomach got to your skin, it would burn a hole in it. The stomach produces cells faster than the acid burns them off. You get a new stomach every three days or so. If this didn't happen, your stomach would digest itself.

A sneeze comes out at around 160 km/hour, a cough at 80 km/hour. Our nerve impulses travel at 400 km/sec.

I could go on and on, but you get the idea. Our bodies are pretty special pieces of super-advanced technology. Look after your body and you will get many, many truly enjoyable free trips around the sun. A strong, healthy body can be quite an asset for the journey we call life, and the sub journey we all have to take, called learning.

I have never been able to study too well when I have had a headache or a stomach problem. The chances are you will not be able to either. To keep this piece of advanced organic technology in shape and make sure it doesn't get defeated by a small mathematical theorem or intimidated by random bits of organic chemistry, there are a few crucial things you should watch out for:

- Make sure you drink enough water.
- Eat good, healthy, fresh food.
- Get enough sleep.
- Exercise regularly.
- Know how to bust stress.
- Maintain personal hygiene.

Water

Our bodies are more than 60 per cent water; our brains are around 80 per cent water. Drinking enough good quality water is supremely important for good health. If you are lucky enough to stay near a fresh water stream, just drink that water. It's the best water in the world.

If not that, then take water from a well or a bore well. This water, after being boiled and then cooled, is the next best thing.

Regardless of what various advertisers claim, avoid reverse osmosis (RO) water filters and bottled water. These kill the vitality inherent in the water and most of the benefits of water are lost.

A glass of water as soon as you wake up in the morning and one before going to bed every night can resolve many health issues and prevent many more from ever happening.

If you work in an air-conditioned environment, or have a very sedentary lifestyle, don't drink more than three litres. Otherwise, it is advisable to keep yourself hydrated by having around four litres of water every day. This is a rule of thumb; for different body types and environments, the daily requirements will vary. Drinking a glass of water half an hour before meals is a great habit. Do not drink water during meals and for about half an hour to an hour after meals. This greatly aids your digestion and prevents you from eating more than you should.

Adding a few pieces of cucumber and a slice of lemon to a pitcher of water and letting it sit for a few hours greatly alkalizes the water.

This alkalized water is fantastic for your body. Many aches and pains and various diseases, gastrointestinal issues in particular, can be resolved by drinking this water throughout the day.

Food

'The journey from the head to the heart is just a few inches, but I took the scenic route via the stomach.' There is nothing quite as satisfying as a fresh, well-made healthy meal. After a lot of research and talking to many doctors and nutritionists, and being completely vegetarian for more than twenty-five years, I have come to the conclusion that a sensible vegetarian diet really brings the glow of health in the body and sharpens the memory and intellect.

There are quite a few volumes written about the benefits of vegetarian food for our bodies, so I won't go into much detail here and encourage you to do your own research. Here are some startling bits of information from a lot of my own research to start you off.

Vegetarian diets can prevent, reverse and dramatically reduce the risk of heart disease, many types of cancers, obesity, stroke, diabetes, almost all food-borne illnesses, constipation, haemorrhoids, IBS and a plethora of other terrible diseases. 51 per cent of our planet's surface today is used by the meat industry to grow and breed livestock – billions and billions of animals. We lose, on average, one acre of rainforests every second; they are being burned down to create space to grow food for the ever growing population of livestock. Keep in mind that in one square mile of rainforest, there are more species than in the entire US of A. If this is not stopped, it is forecast that by 2050 there will be no forests left at all. The meat industry is the biggest cause of extinction of species, depletion of rainforests and the second biggest cause of pollution (after power generation). The meat industry causes 40 per cent more pollution than all the transport systems of the planet. If unchecked it will become a serious threat to life as we know it on our beautiful planet.

Have you ever been hungry? You have that gnawing feeling in your stomach and can't wait to get to food … imagine dying of that! More than 750 million people die every year because of hunger and hunger-related issues. If all the citizens of the United States of America went vegetarian – and that's just 4 per cent of the world's population – there would be enough food for more than a billion people. Imagine the cornucopia of plenty we would have if everyone went vegetarian! There would be no more hunger, or death related to hunger, even if our current population doubled!

If all the water on our planet could be compressed into a one-litre bottle, then the amount of drinking water available is only what would fit in the cap of that bottle. Water is super precious. The meat industry consumes and pollutes humungous amounts of water. A vegetarian could leave the shower on, all day, 365 days a year and yet not consume as much water as a person who has meat in their diet. To put this in perspective: to save 5,000 litres of water, don't flush your toilet for six months, or don't shower for three months, or skip eating a hamburger for one meal!

To Save **5000** Liters of water

Don't shower for 3 months

OR

Don't flush your toilet for 6 months

OR

Don't eat 1 hamburger

Because animals raised for meat are reared in horrible conditions and in incredibly cramped quarters, farmers will resort to anything to stop a disease cropping up and decimating their entire herd. They inject animals with tons of antibiotics to prevent infections. Humans consume these antibiotics when they eat the flesh of the animals. This makes it very hard for doctors to treat diseases because the bugs are already resistant to the antibiotics that have been acquired through eating meat, floating around in the bloodstream.

The meat industry has killed more people than every single war, automobile accident and natural disaster in the last 100 years.

Finally, eat vegetarian food to show your compassion. The billions and billions of animals slaughtered in the most heinous ways have no voice. If you do eat meat, for the sake of those creatures that suffer horrifically at the hands of humanity, please switch to a vegetarian diet. See if in your heart you can speak up for those who have no voice to speak. Graduate to a plant-based diet. Encourage others around you as well to eat vegetarian food.

More than a decade ago, I was teaching some courses in the US. I made the same plea to my students: that they go vegetarian. They readily agreed. After a week, I got a phone call from a very distressed student. He said that he had been eating only vegetarian food and was now feeling really sick. I was surprised, and so I asked him what he had eaten in the previous week. 'Vegetarian food like you said,' came the reply; 'I have been eating French fries!'

That's when I added the word 'sensible' to my statement. To have a healthy body, eat a *sensible* vegetarian diet. In this sense, things have changed a lot in recent years. The West is realizing the folly of meat-based diets and is slowly but surely turning towards plants for their food. Unfortunately, the trend seems to be reversing in India and other developing nations, where meat-eating has become a kind of a status symbol. There is an urgent need to educate the masses about the harrowing effects that meat has on the human body and on the ecosystems of our planet and encourage them to go back to vegetarian food.

So what's a healthy diet? What should you be eating? When should you eat? And what's the stuff you should avoid?

Answering these questions at length will make for a series of books. So I will simply list a few guidelines here and leave the rest to you and Google.

A balanced diet should have carbohydrates, fats, proteins, minerals, vitamins and fibres.

The golden rule is to eat fresh, preferably local, minimally processed organic food. Mix and match tastes and colours in every meal. Eat a lot of raw and minimally cooked food.

Never skip breakfast. That's the time of the day when the metabolism is at its strongest. Start your day with a bowl of fruits. Have three to five different types if you can. It's much better to have fruit than fruit juice, even if it's freshly prepared fruit juice. Wait about half an hour after your fruit and then have breakfast.

After that, a few small meals are better than two big meals. Dinner should be light. It is best not to eat anything after 8.30 p.m. Ideally, there needs to be a three-hour gap between your last meal and going to bed.

It's fantastic to end the day with a glass of milk. Make sure the milk you are having is that of the Indian 'desi' cow. It has A2 milk protein and is great for human consumption. The milk of the Jersey cow and other hybrid cows contains A1 protein and is unfit for human consumption. Ayurveda says that milk is best absorbed during the night. It is rich in absorbable calcium. It contains tryptophan, which helps us get good sleep. It keeps the body hydrated through the night.

Make sure that the grains to veggies ratio is 1:2 or more. Grains become superfoods when they are sprouted; more proteins, vitamins and minerals become available. Sprouting increases the fibre content by almost three times and lowers the gluten content. Grains such as millet, amaranth, quinoa, barley and ragi are healthier alternatives to wheat.

If you like to snack, have legumes, sprouts, beans, dry fruits, pumpkin seeds and sunflower seeds in small portions.

A big problem is that what we actually eat and what we think we are eating rarely match. Read ingredient labels carefully. The main ingredient is always listed first, followed by the one with the next highest percentage and so on. You think you are drinking juice, but if the ingredients say 'water, sugar, fruit pulp', you are actually drinking sugar water with a tiny bit of fruit pulp thrown in mainly for colour.

White refined flour, white sugar and white polished rice are perhaps the worst things that we routinely eat. They cause havoc in our bodies and put our bodies in a vicious loop of craving for more.

Processed food, especially tinned food, has next to nothing in it, nutritionally speaking. You might just be consuming the equivalent of tasty cardboard.

Our bodies love to be alkaline inside. Unfortunately, most of the food we eat is acidic in nature. It is recommended that we have around 70 to 80 per cent alkaline food and just 20 per cent acidic food.

A chart listing alkaline and acidic food for your reference is given as Illustration 12.

Say an absolutely emphatic no to alcohol, smoking or recreational drugs. Besides shaving years off your life, these things add ridiculous amounts of misery to your life and to the lives of people around you.

Eating your meals more or less at the same time every day can be a game changer as far as fitness and health is concerned. Don't follow any diet that guarantees weight loss or a 'great' body in a few weeks. Getting a great body requires time and commitment, and anything that is claimed to be a 'quick fix' most definitely is not.

Check Chapter 18 for some of my favourite recipes. You will find even more on my blog www.bawandinesh.in.

Sleep

Sleep is the longest uninterrupted activity that a human body routinely does. Getting a good night's sleep is a blessing and makes a tremendous impact on the quality of your work. The body has a schedule according to which it repairs and rejuvenates itself. Illustration 9 is a chart that shows the rhythm that the body follows.

There are systems in the body that secrete – or stop secreting – certain hormones that maintain bodily functions at different levels of readiness. For example, at 10.30 p.m., bowel movement is restricted while at 8.30 a.m., bowel movement is encouraged.

Between 11.00 p.m. and around 3.00 a.m. is the time for deep sleep. This is when the body really pulls its socks up and gets to work, repairing the wear and tear it has experienced. If you are awake during this time, there is no chance for the body to fix itself and over time disease sets in. Fortunately, the body is amazingly elastic and given half a chance will manage to fix itself over time. Even years of abuse can be fixed with relative ease if food and sleep patterns are taken care of.

Recent research shows that our brain clears out its trash during sleep! The brain uses about 20 per cent of all the energy the body produces. When energy is used, there is always junk created in the form of toxic molecules. I call it Brain Poo. Accumulating Brain Poo over the years is an open invitation to diseases like Alzheimer's.

Ideally, the CSF (cerebrospinal fluid) should be able to drain it out, but when you are awake, the space in the brain is literally jammed with activity. This doesn't allow the CSF to do its job efficiently. When you are sleeping, the interstitial space (the fluid area surrounding the cells of a tissue) swells to more than 20 per cent of its size when you are awake. Some scientists claim it can be up to 60 per cent.

This provides the required room for the CSF to play the janitor and clear out all the deadly waste that's been generated during the day's mental activity. It also allows the CSF to reach deeper within the brain, to places it simply cannot access when the brain is active.

Going for an exam sleep deprived, after an all-night session of cramming, translates into super sluggish neural activity. You may even forget what you already know because your brain is full of poo!

To cut a long story short, everyone should be sleeping at least six to eight hours, not more than nine hours and making sure that they are in deep slumber between the hours of 11.00 p.m. and 3.00 a.m. This will ensure many years of great health, a sharper intellect, a physically cleaner brain and a keener mind.

Exercise

Exercise is really good for you. Our bodies adapt themselves to our lifestyle. A dancer's body is very different from a body builder's. The body speaks volumes about how you are living your life. The right type of exercise will ensure that all the systems of the body are maintained in peak condition.

Walk or cycle instead of taking a car or riding a bike. Climb up and down the stairs instead of using the lift. Give your body a chance to move and it will reward you with fantastic health. Jogging, swimming and, of course, going to the gym and working out are fabulous things you can do for your body.

The surya namaskars are the most complete set of asanas we know. When done slowly, they greatly increase balance, strength and coordination. When done fast, they increase flexibility, stamina and fat loss and enhance cardiovascular functioning.

Doing them on a regular basis also increases your intuitive powers. Lord Krishna was said to lead the Pandava army through the surya namaskars every morning, and many claim that this set of asanas are the secret behind the superhuman strength and flexibility of the Pandava brothers. It's best to study this from a qualified yoga teacher. Please use the text and images in Chapter 19 as references rather than for actual learning.

Apart from the surya namaskars, we have created a set of eight exercises that focus on separate body parts to give them a quick work out. We feel that if you do just this much consistently, you will have done a lot for your body to stay fit and healthy.

These are simple exercises that anyone can do. Keep in mind though that doing these will not get you a body like Arnold Schwarzenegger's. These exercises will keep you pretty fit and hopefully carve out a pretty good V shape over time. As before, I would recommend that you exercise with a good trainer and use the images and instructions in Chapter 22 more as references rather than for learning.

A word of warning: do not take any 'bulk me up' steroids. Chemicals like those are simply not good for you and cause all sorts of complications.

Staying fit is not rocket science. Eat well. Get enough sleep. Exercise regularly. You will have a great body.

Apart from water, food, rest and exercise, knowing how to bust stress is a life skill totally worth acquiring. Sri Sri Ravi Shankar has a neat definition of stress. He says that stress means too much to do, too little time and not enough energy.

Increasing your capacity to do things and increasing your energy levels are the keys to beating stress. Good food eaten on time, plenty of hydration throughout the day, getting enough sleep (on time) and regular exercise will make sure you don't get stressed easily. The mind however plays a much bigger part than the body in the fight against stress. When you have learnt to meditate and are regularly practising meditation, stress will hardly touch you. Meditation is not something you can learn from a book. You will need to find a qualified teacher to teach you how to meditate. Personally, I would recommend Art of Living's Sudarshan Kriya and Sahaj Samadhi Meditation techniques. These are time-tested and have benefitted millions, including Dinesh and myself. There could be other techniques to meditate as well, but since I have not learnt or practiced any of them, I do not consider myself qualified to comment on them.

One little piece of advice though ... once you have learnt how to meditate, don't go shopping for more techniques. A river cannot be crossed in a dozen boats. You have to choose one and stick to it and have faith that it will take you across the river to your destination.

Don't forget to maintain personal hygiene. Showering, brushing your teeth, wearing clean clothes and all the other things that our mothers and grandmothers have lectured us about are pretty important as well.

A healthy, fit body may not guarantee a mind like Einstein's, but life definitely becomes easier to handle ... and perhaps quantum mechanics will not look quite so intimidating.

ATTITUDE: STUDYING FOR KNOWLEDGE

In ancient India, the Gurukul system encouraged a lively inquisitiveness and a healthy respect for knowledge. The ancients were unthinkably advanced; their prowess was legendary even in their own time. Today, we find ancient scrolls depicting flying machines and warheads, treatises on advanced mathematics, plastic surgery, astronomy and a myriad of other arts and sciences. They made rust-proof iron, something modern science has still not been able to produce; even today, some of those iron pillars survive, defying both pollution and acid rain without any trace of rust.

Somewhere down the line, because of invasions and the influence of the West and to a much smaller degree, the refusal of the 'pundits' to share their knowledge and wisdom with the masses, India lost her most valuable treasure – Knowledge.

Until the early part of the twentieth century, even in the West, people went for higher education because their subjects fascinated them. They were passionate about what they were studying and intensely curious about the world around them.

No one went to university to get a job or to be better qualified for marriage!

Most young people today study for one or more of the following reasons:

1. To get 'ahead' in life
2. Because their parents want them to
3. To have a standing in society
4. To be with their friends
5. To get a job
6. Because they have nothing else to do
7. To get married

When I was in the Grade 11, I had a scientific calculator that also had a space invaders game in it; the one where you repeatedly press a key and things on the screen burst into a multitude of pixels. And you get a strange sort of satisfaction. My sister was in Grade 3 at that time and she loved to play the game.

Once, after a long session of annihilated aliens, she suddenly came to me and said, 'The "za" sign is not working. It's broken.'

'Za?' I asked.

'Yes, the "za" sign is not working.'

The za sign turned out to be the equal to (=) sign. Wondering why?

She had learnt the multiplication tables that way.

2 ones are two ($2 \times 1 = 2$)
2 twos are four ($2 \times 2 = 4$)
2 threes are six ($2 \times 3 = 6$)

Say it out aloud and you will see why '=' becomes 'za'!

She had learnt the multiplication tables without knowing what multiplication meant. Despite knowing the tables by heart, she had no idea what it was she had learnt!

For most people, this style of 'learning' goes on till graduation, and sometimes even beyond. Most educational institutions around the country are steadily churning out people who are 'educated', but have almost no idea about their subjects. I call them the educated unemployable. Who will give them jobs? They possess a worthless piece of paper that says they know stuff that they don't.

Here's another example. I was pretty good at French and used to help my teacher grade papers. There was this one person who had submitted a near perfect paper except there was one answer I didn't understand. For a question that asked, 'What is a croissant?', they had written, 'Un croissant est un patisserie leger en forme 53 de croissant de lune.' I didn't know what to make of the 53. Otherwise the sentence meant, 'A croissant is a light pastry shaped like the crescent of the moon', and was perfectly right.

When I showed it to my French teacher, she started to laugh … While learning the answers by rote, this person had even memorized the page number which was at the bottom right of the textbook.

Despite scoring 85 per cent or more in the subject, I don't think he actually knew much about it. Of what use is such education? Studies have become drudgery. Boring. People look at their books and want to puke. Or go to sleep. There is little to no interest in what they are doing and the only goal seems to pass or to get good grades.

It's all about learning without understanding, fiercely competing for better marks instead of focusing on better understanding.

Once, I was struggling with a concept and went to a friend who claimed that he knew it. He looked at the problem I was stuck on and said, 'Oh, I don't understand that one either, and I just mugged it up.' This attitude is a loser's attitude: learning something by rote without understanding it. Learning to simply get through an exam. Learning just to get good marks. Learning to vomit accurately.

The first and most important rule of studying is:

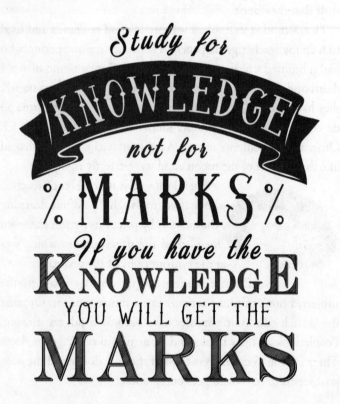

Study for
KNOWLEDGE
not for
% MARKS %
If you have the
KNOWLEDGE
YOU WILL GET THE
MARKS

If your study of a subject doesn't fill you with wonder, or at least with interest, then you are doing something wrong. You have missed the point. The greatest human minds, the keenest of intellects have over hundreds of years studied and created the books that we study from. The distilled versions of years of toil, triumphs, frustrations and flashes of inspiration of countless geniuses over the ages make up a modern textbook. A feeling of reverence, like entering some great cathedral, is what you should feel when you open a book to study. Definitely not the feelings of disgust and angst. When you open your mind to the possibility of studying to understand, to learn, to grapple with your subject, only then has true education begun. When this happens, a feeling of excitement will come when you start your work. You will actually look forward to it!

No subject can be boring or uninteresting. How can it be? A genius will not dedicate his life to something that's boring. The root cause of students hating their subjects is listless, uninspired teaching and badly written textbooks. Many professors should be jailed for the cold-hearted murder of the subjects they teach. Even so, a badly written book or a teacher who sucks should not push you away from your love for the subject. A true student is one who can love their work in spite of pathetic teaching; who can celebrate the glory of the knowledge they are imbibing.

I, too, went through the same, mostly useless education system that you are (possibly) going through. But I used something called a library for doing things other than sleep. Now, I use something called the internet for learning more instead of just for Facebook.

When you have thoroughly understood your subject – when you have grasped the fundamentals and are confident about your knowledge of it – then, education has truly happened.

When you graduate, society is going to rely on you for the knowledge that your degree proclaims you to have. An architect cannot say he doesn't know how to design ceilings. A doctor cannot say he doesn't know where the kidneys are. If you are only studying for great marks, you may possibly get a head start in life but the people who truly understand their subjects will quickly overtake you.

Having said all of that, I must tell you that I am not against learning by heart. You will need to memorize a lot of information so that you can work at speed, and there is nothing wrong with that as long as you have understood what it is you are mugging up. I am not against getting great grades either. In fact, when you have knowledge of your subject, it will become incredibly difficult for you to get bad grades. But it is not true the other way around. Great grades may not mean you truly understand. Great grades may not mean you are actually educated.

This attitude shift needs to happen inside you.

Be a winner. Study for Knowledge, not for marks. Get an Education, not a degree.

A note to parents:

When your child comes home from an exam, there is a question that most parents ask. 'How many marks did you get?' is the most common; or perhaps, 'Did you pass?' depending on the perceived ability of the child.

This question conveys to the child that you are not interested in what they have learnt, how much they have grasped. What you are communicating is that you mostly care about the marks or if they passed or failed. If this happens enough times, the child lets go of their innate curiosity, their built-in ability to actually learn and starts to focus on what will make the parents happy: marks.

PLEASE stop asking this question. When the child comes home, ask, 'What did you learn today?' and then, listen. Then the education that has started in school has a chance to continue at home, and your child has a fighting chance for real success.

A true blossoming of the intellect becomes a distinct possibility. Do this as a favour to your child, for your country and for our beautiful planet.

BUT I HATE MATH!

Were you born with an inbuilt hatred of mathematics hardwired into your DNA? Did you pop out of your mother's womb crying, 'Waaahhhhhh, waaahhhhhh, I hate maths, waaahhhhhhh!'?

For most of us this is not the case.

As children, we find the world fascinating and are awed by its beauty. We want to explore everything and know as much as possible. In the senseless race to get good marks, teachers and parents – and possibly the worst culprits, the coaching classes – systematically extinguish all curiosity and wonder.

By the time you hit the fifth or sixth standard, studying already feels like the big burden. It is around that time most people encounter a terror of a teacher; one who believes that learning can only happen through fear. We are too young and naïve to hate that teacher, so we end up hating that subject instead. For most people, it's a scar that will not heal until they understand that it was just the teacher who sucked and not the subject itself. Understand this fact. Give the subject another chance. Don't let that past haunt your present and your future. It is true that some of us simply might not have the aptitude for certain fields. That problem will fade a little as you get into higher studies, since you can choose your subjects more precisely. Until that happy day, simply grit your teeth and bear it and get through with it.

One subject I didn't like was organic chemistry. I suffered through it in the first year of my B.Sc. Then in the second year, I took physics and maths and was done with it. We had quite a celebration when I had given the last chemistry exam of my life!

In general however if we decide to like a subject, it grows on us and we can unravel the mysteries and wonders inherent in it.

Then statistics came into my life. There was no escape from it. It was very much a part of learning to be a mathematician. Nothing else has given me as many sleepless nights. I used to utterly abhor, detest and despise statistics. I remember thinking that if I had a time machine I would have gone back in time and made sure that this loathsome subject never even began!

Fortunately for me, around that time, I did an Art of Living course, and one of the things the teacher said was, 'What you like and not like is your decision. And you can change it any time. Take responsibility for what's happening in your mind and in your life. Only you can fix it!'

It was then that the possibility of actually liking stats opened up for me.

That night, after classes, I sat with my big fat stats textbook and told myself: 'I love statistics!'

I read a few pages, but still thought, 'Yuck.' This was not working. My mind said, 'No ... nonononono no! Please don't inflict this on me!'

I said to myself, 'I am bigger than my mind; I LOOOOOVE statistics! It's my decision! I love it, I love it, I love it!'

Went over a few more pages – ugh, yuck ewwww…

I LOVEEEEE Statistics!

Aaaarrrgghhhh…

I   LLLLLLLLOOOOOOOOOVVVVVVEEEEEEE STATISTICS!!!!

And then, while flipping pages in sheer helplessness, I suddenly came upon a box on one of the pages that talked about probability and horses and winning money in races! And I thought, 'Hmmm, that looks interesting, maybe there is some formula for getting rich', and started to read that part. The problem was that I had gone, 'Ugh, ewww and yuck', for the past seventy or so pages, and so I didn't understand most of what was going on.

I went back and started reading the parts I had skipped to be able to understand this interesting part … and the next time I looked up, the sun had risen and I had fallen in love with statistics! For the record, I hold a master's degree in mathematics from IIT Bombay, with a specialization in statistics and operations research.

A decision to enjoy the subject and give it a chance is the second rule for studying effectively. It is a very personal decision. Many, many young people who used to hate a particular subject, found that very same subject suddenly become super interesting… As soon as they managed to flip that little switch in their own minds.

Another way of looking at it is this. In life there are going to be some things you will simply have to do. There is just no escape from them. So now, do you have any choice in the matter? Most will reply, 'No, if we have to do it anyway, then where is the choice?'

I say there is always a choice.

Even when you HAVE to do something, there is a choice; it is just that the question changes. If you have to do it, the choice is between, 'I will be happy doing it' and 'I will be miserable doing it'. The intelligent choose the option with happy in it.

Another objection comes swiftly along. 'But I simply can't concentrate.' Or even, 'I don't know HOW to concentrate.'

Hmmm … really?

Ever watched a really nice movie? One you so thoroughly enjoyed that it had you on the edge of your seat with excitement or rolling on the floor laughing? For the two and a half hours of that movie, did you think of anything else? Did your mind wander at all? Weren't you utterly, fully, completely focused on what was happening on that screen?

You DO know how to focus and concentrate. As soon as it's time to study you somehow manage to forget that skill.

When do you need to focus? When you don't like what you are doing … right?

When you are enjoying yourself watching a movie, or eating ice cream, or playing a game, or screaming your head off with excitement on a roller coaster, the focus comes all by itself. But bring out that economics textbook and your focus does a vanishing act.

And whose decision is it to like a subject?

Decide to enjoy your studies, and you may actually start looking forward to curling up with your books. It helps to schedule short study periods of difficult subjects. Say, 20-30 minutes of completely uninterrupted focused work with something you just have to do, but may not want to do. As you build up your knowledge about the subject and start to understand even just a little bit of it, you gain confidence and can work even longer. In time, the boredom and drudgery associated with your work will vanish. If you are lucky, you may even develop an actual interest in your work.

A TALE OF TWO TEACHERS

At my school (Don Bosco, Matunga), we had something called a calendar that every student carried. It was basically a smallish, blue-coloured book that we could use as a diary, with space for stuff that we wanted to write, our marks in various tests and exams and the 'Remarks' page.

On this page, sadistic teachers would leave notes about us when we didn't do something they wanted us to do or, alternatively, *did* do something they didn't want us to. Students then had to get these notes signed by equally sadistic parents who would come up with very creative ways of making life miserable in exchange for their signatures. I was too bhola to even think of forging signatures, and besides, my parents had supernatural powers when it came to finding out stuff you really wanted to keep hidden!

That's where my grandparents came in. My granddad would look at the remark, raise his eyebrows and then silently sign it, almost as if it was an autograph book. Life revolved around the Remarks page. You couldn't get more than twelve remarks in a year, or the principal would summon your parents, and that would make life truly miserable for quite a prolonged period of time. But there were lighter moments too; one of my teachers, Mrs Sampat, who was a little English-challenged, would write 'Homework not done' in the Remarks page regardless of the offence.

When I look back now, I see that the weak teachers – the ones who couldn't hold a class's attention or simply didn't know how to teach the subject – and were just doing a 'job' – relished this power that they wielded over us hapless students who had to suffer them. The really good teachers, the ones who bring a smile to the face and dampness to the eyes even when we think of them thirty years later, never ever left me a Remark. They didn't need to discipline us at all. They commanded our respect and love, they never demanded it. They were the ones who we looked at and thought, 'I would love to become like this person.' I guess the others just served as examples of how not to be!

Here are two stories. One of a good teacher who became great and another of a truly brilliant teacher who made me feel great!

Dr Narayan*

Towards the end of my time at IIT, I had opted for a course in advanced statistics. This was when I had already done quite a bit of introspection and had decided that I wouldn't worry about grades any more. I was just going to enjoy the process of studying for the sake of studying and amass as much knowledge as I possibly could. No one else had opted for this course, so I was the only student. It was like having private tuitions. Dr

---

* Name changed to protect identity

Narayan was a pretty good teacher. I thoroughly enjoyed the subject under his expert guidance and was becoming pretty good at it.

The coursework for that course was just an eighty-page textbook, with eight or nine theorems. The proof of each theorem was long and winding, sometimes running into seven to eight printed pages. Each theorem was followed by a few exercises that were applications. These exercises really tested if you truly understood the theorem.

I submitted my assignments on time, clearly and legibly written, and was the epitome of a good student, at least for this class. I did all the problems my professor gave me, though I have to say that being the only student there, I couldn't have copied stuff out even if I wanted to.

By the end of the semester, Dr Narayan had a very good idea of how much I had understood of his subject. I had also asked him, for the end-of-semester exam, to consider not testing me on the proofs of the theorems; he knew I had understood the concepts well and that I really saw no point in learning the whole thing by rote.

He would nod and smile, and I believed that he agreed with me.

The end-of-semester exam approached, and I went to the exam hall full of confidence, ready to tackle some interesting applications of all those theorems I had learnt. Dr Narayan had other ideas. He had set a paper with forty-two marks worth of theorem proofs and only eight marks of applications. I answered eight marks worth of applications and proved the theorems to the best of my recall ability. I had memorized some key results and their derivations but had definitely not prepared for a full-on assault on the prowess of my memory.

I was awarded an E grade for my efforts. E meant I had failed the course, but I could give a re-exam in a few days at a mutually convenient time and had high chances of clearing the course.

I went to his office and confronted him. I politely asked him why he had given me an E when I clearly deserved a B, if not an A. He knew all that I knew. My knowledge of the subject was quite impeccable and I really did deserve a good grade – definitely not an E.

He said, 'I only go by what you have written on the answer sheet. Your answers do not convince me that you know the subject. If I give you a good grade, I would be answerable to all the other students before you who I failed with similar levels of answering.'

I countered, 'But you know that I know my stuff!'

He agreed but stuck to his point of going only by what was written on the answer sheet. He was gracious enough to ask me when I wanted my re-exam. I asked for four or five days. He agreed.

I worked hard for the next few days and learnt the entire textbook by heart. It was just eightyish-odd pages anyway, and the theorems were fairly straightforward. It was quite easy to do it because I had already grasped the subject and the material was very familiar to me.

When I went for the re-exam, I utterly ignored the questions he had asked and simply wrote out the entire textbook. After I had finished, I wrote with a red marker pen on the last page:

'THIS DOES NOT MEAN I UNDERSTAND ANY OF THE ABOVE!'

I turned in my answer sheet and went back to my hostel. In less than fifteen minutes I got a phone call from Dr Narayan asking me to come see him at his office.

He was a changed man. He was deeply apologetic. He said he had never ever considered if his students had truly understood and grasped their subjects while grading them. He said he felt foolish and I felt sorry for him. We had long discussions after that about what it means to teach and who deserves good grades and who don't.

I never had another course with him, but some of my juniors told me that he tells my story to his students to inspire them to study for knowledge and not just for marks.

He was a good teacher who transformed into a truly brilliant teacher. It feels good to know that I contributed big time to this transformation.

Dr D.V. Pai

Along came a subject called Real Analysis.

I used to hate that subject because when I had first studied it, for my bachelor's degree, I had studied with a terrible professor who managed to make everyone in the class utterly detest the subject. I was a fool. I actually hated the professor and had managed to transfer my hatred of him to the subject.

Since I had terrible memories of the subject, I didn't attend any lectures and didn't bother studying it at all. I got six on thirty in my mid-semester exam. It was one of those subjects I simply wanted to scrape through.

One sunny afternoon, I got a phone call at my hostel. It was Dr Pai, who was teaching the course. Could I please come and see him in his office soon? My heart was beating quite wildly, but we arranged to meet within the next hour or so. I always like to get unpleasant things over as soon as possible.

After shaving, showering and putting on some (relatively) clean clothes, I did the Sudarshan Kriya and walked to the maths department, each step making me more and more apprehensive about the firing I was about to get.

Thinking about what he would say and what excuse I would then give was playing havoc in my mind. 'Live in the present moment' did flash through my thoughts a few times, but it didn't help much.

There was a storm in my mind as I climbed the stairs to Dr Pai's office. I said an intense heartfelt prayer in my head and knocked on his door.

'Come in, Mr Batliwala.'

His voice was very pleasant. Some hope flickered, and as I entered I saw him smile as he looked up from some papers. Somehow, he managed to put me at ease in the first ten seconds that I was there in his office.

'Please sit down.'

What he said to me afterwards is etched in my memory. He said it gently, slowly and matter-of-factly:

'In the thirty years that I have taught here, I have never failed a student because I have always known that there is no such thing as a bad student in IIT-B, only a bad teacher. If a student does badly, it's the teacher who could not ignite the passion for the subject in the student.

'I do not expect you to come to my lectures. But I do expect you to know your subject. You have not done well in the mid-semesters, so clearly you cannot do this on your own. I loved the way you played the piano ...' (He had heard me during PAF, The Performing Arts Festival, where the entire student body gets together for a few weeks and puts up a grand production showing off all the talents they have) 'and someone who can play so well can easily learn Real Analysis.'

He then continued even more gently:

'Will you please give me a chance to teach this subject to you?'

By this time, my eyes were wet. He smiled a big smile and sighed. 'Will you have a cup of tea?'

'I will come to each and every lecture, sir,' I promised, and I did for the rest of the semester, and his eyes always twinkled when he saw me. We shared a secret!

After all these years, if you are reading this, Dr Pai, please know that you were one of the big reasons I stuck it out at IIT-B and completed my degree. Thank you very, very much for being part of my life ... and oh yes, I still love to read up Real Analysis!

EMERGENCY STUDYING

There are two ways to study: leisurely studying and emergency studying.

It is supremely preferable to study leisurely and we will talk about how to do that at length in a bit. First, I must confess that as a student, there were many times that I was faced with the inevitability of emergency studying. The type when you stay up all night and cram as much as possible into your brain.

This becomes harder as you go, because your brain already feels like it is bursting at the seams. Cerebrospinal fluid seems to be dripping out of your ears.

It is at this point that most people realize that the evening is too beautiful to waste on studying. So, you take a walk/exercise/play the piano, whatever, until you simply can't put off sitting in front of those photocopied notes (of course you attended very few lectures) and with a deep breath, begin working.

You sail through the first 15-20 pages or so. Then you stretch, yawn and make the fatal mistake. You count the number of pages left: One, two, three, four … thirty-five, thirty-six, thirty-seven … aarrgghh, sixty-one, sixty-two, sixty-three!

You get on the phone and start to ask your friends, all of whom are also studying from the same notes, how many pages they have finished. Twelve, sixteen, twenty-six; all are acceptable answers. Until that one guy hurriedly says, 'I am in such a soup, I am utterly unprepared, have only finished my second revision!'

Feelings of doom and gloom dawn.

To recover from the depression, you head to the mess downstairs and have your cup of tea or coffee. And discuss the sheer futility and pointlessness of exams and life in general with other similarly depressed people. A wide range of philosophical debates happen at this time as kindred souls exchange their views on the Universe, God, quantum physics and string theory, merits of vadapav over misalpav, spirulina as a protein substitute, did Ravana really have ten heads, how to murder a professor and get away with it, making easy money, the state of the country and the corruption in the government and other such topics which no one ever thinks of except in the night before an impending exam.

Wearily you make your way back to your desk. It's been three hours since you began studying, and you have only finished twenty pages. Oh God! Oh God!! Oh God!!!

You update your status on Facebook to: 'Screwed.'

Some pages later, a brilliant idea strikes. 'Why don't I go through the question papers from the last few years and see what's been regularly asked?' Armed with a marker pen or three, you start making signs on the notes. Your previously black and white notes are transformed into glorious technicolor with 'imp's, 'vimp's, 'vvimp's, 'mimp's all over the page, with as many stars, moons and other assorted symbols that you can come up with.

You turn to the place where there is maximum colour and say to yourself, 'OK, if I get this topic done, that's fifteen marks!' Only, that topic is on page fifty-six, and once you start to read, it makes little to no sense because you have skipped around thirty-five pages in between where you were and this topic.

You sigh and get back to page twenty-five. It's been another hour and you have only done five more pages...

Then the mind stuff kicks in. The first thoughts are about how stupid and idiotic you are. 'How foolish I am! I should have studied from the beginning of the semester. Then I wouldn't be in this mess. I am useless! Hopeless! Pathetic! Next time I won't make this mistake. Next time, I will be regular in class and be asleep at 10.00 p.m. the night before the exam. Next time, next time, next time...'

Then the morbid thoughts come. 'Suppose I fail? Dad will kill me! Worse, he will cut my pocket money! If I don't have enough money, how am I going to patao my girlfriend?! She will think I am cheap and go off with that Sandeep/Rajeev/Venky who has been eyeing her. How will I continue life without her? My life will be ruined. I HAVE TO PASS!!!'

Five more pages, if you are lucky.

Then a fantasy arrives. Tomorrow the exam will get cancelled. There might be a war between India and Pakistan. The pope might die. There could be an earthquake. The professor might die. There could be a bomb scare. Something will happen; something SHOULD happen!

Aarrgghh!

Somehow you make it through the night and manage to get to the exam hall, where you puke half-baked ideas of whatever you can recall on to the answer sheet. Then, you go to a temple immediately after to pray for redemption.

And every time you need to do this emergency studying, you do almost exactly the same thing.

There was one memorable subject in which I didn't even know the names of the mathematical symbols being used. I hated the professor and refused to go for his lectures. I didn't know anything about the subject at all. That night I spent lying on the terrace, waiting for a shooting star so I could make a wish to clear that paper. I was in such a hopeless situation that this seemed to be the only logical thing to do.

I did see a shooting star at around 2 a.m. I made my wish.

Fortunately for me, the professor hated me as much as I hated him and he didn't want to see me in his class again the next semester. He actually passed me! (This, however, is not a recommended strategy to try the night before an exam.)

There is one critical thing we do that leads us into this mess. The utter refusal to accept that there is an exam tomorrow and you are not prepared for it.

When you have not accepted the fact that is staring you in the face, then you will either complain about the situation or be in denial about it. No sensible action is possible when you are in denial or in complain mode.

When you have to do emergency studying, the first thing to do is accept the fact that you are not prepared. Once acceptance comes, then there is higher probability of intelligent action.

When there is acceptance, you will not waste time counting pages, having pointless philosophical discussions with tea, phoning or Facebooking, sitting and blaming yourself or fantasizing, etc.

If you have truly accepted that you are not prepared, all you will do is study to the exclusion of everything else. Just sit there and work.

For me, the critical fatal thing was counting the number of pages left. Who cares how many pages are left? Forget about it. Just sit there and work. Do your best and leave the rest to whoever you believe your guardian angel to be.

I have found that when I have this attitude, I get through what I have to do faster, and at the end, have a saner mind. This helps big time, especially when it comes to answering the questions on the actual exam.

Rashmin, a great friend of mine, tells the ultimate emergency studying story:

'I was going through my Organization of Commerce (OC) textbook an hour before the exam at the exam hall. The guy sitting next to me asked, "Are you a CA foundation student?"

'I replied, "No, FYJC (First Year Junior College)."'

'Soon, he had an expression of confusion mixed with alarm on his face, peppered with shock and liberally seasoned with fear when I then asserted that the exam that day was OC, not Marathi.

'In a few moments the very same expression jumped from his face to mine when we realized that it was me who was going through the wrong textbook, not him.

'Suddenly shifting from Organization of Commerce to Marathi was supremely difficult. An hour left for the exam in which I needed thirty-six marks to pass and I did not even remember what the Marathi textbook looked like.

'After winning over thoughts of ending my life, I became capable of functioning somewhat normally. I still remember the three types of people I encountered as I went about telling my tale of woe to whoever cared to listen.

'Type 1: What a fool you are. Why didn't you see the timetable properly? Their tone and demeanour just increased my panic.

'Type 2: Break your hand, leg or something … Get a medical certificate. They will allow you to write the exam later. Solutions of a sort, but to me they felt non workable.

'Type 3: The ones who silently gave me a compassionate look and would quickly go back to their books.

'Then fate intervened and I met Abhay, a very good friend. Looking at my lost-dog expression, he was quick to sense trouble and after getting to know what the problem was, he kept smiling. He was the only one who responded as if there was no problem at all. It made me feel better.

'He said half an hour was more than enough time to study! He was calm and collected. He opened the Marathi textbook to the index page.

'In fifteen minutes he gave me the summaries of all the chapters and poems. He asked me to memorize the names of the authors, poets and characters of each chapter. Thankfully, being a chess player, I had the ability to memorize quickly. The last five minutes he asked me to just chill and relax.

'I was already feeling better and not utterly unprepared for the exam. After meeting Abhay, the last half an hour was completely utilized doing relevant things. He exuded confidence and somehow it started rubbing off on me. There were no stupid questions, no panic and no sympathy. It was just intelligent action.

'During the exam, I gave my 100 per cent, answering whatever I could.

'The results came out. I got exactly thirty-six marks in Marathi. I had passed. Abhay had taught me a very big lesson. He had demonstrated the power of acceptance and being adaptable to changing situations. He gave me hope where there was none. He was a friend who made me feel bigger than my problem.'

Here are a few tips for emergency studying:

1. Accept that you are not prepared.
2. Start as early as possible in the evening.
3. As far as possible, work in a well-lit room that has good ventilation.
4. Don't waste time on pointless activity.
5. Keep all the stuff you need for the exam the next day packed and ready – pens, colour pencils, markers, calculator, etc.
6. Don't bother making a schedule. Your only schedule is work till you can't. Then push it a bit more. Then sleep and wake up early enough that you can go over whatever you have done before the exam.
7. Don't try a 'new' way of studying. Stick with what you know for now.
8. Sit and start to work.
9. Pray. A quick prayer can help in ways you cannot imagine.
10. Don't count the number of pages left. Just work.
11. Don't phone other people; get off Facebook.
12. Keep all the stuff you need handy: your notes, blank sheets, pens, textbooks, whatever.

13. Keep stuff you don't need away from you. There is very little chance that you are going to need to Google something or look it up on the net. So keep that laptop or iPad away from you. Otherwise Facebook, some game, porn or other similar distracting pointless activities might suddenly become a priority. Keep your phone on silent.

14. I found that studying with one or two other people in the same room helped big time. If any one of us lost focus, just looking at the others would bring it back. This cuts both ways – choose whom you are studying with carefully. There are people who will distract you endlessly.

15. Drink water. Not tea, coffee or cola.

16. Eat a light dinner and keep some simple munchies around to take care of hunger pangs. Khakharas with some cheese are a personal favourite.

17. When you start, skim over the entire notes two to three times at least so you get some rough idea of what are you in for. If there is stuff you remember, or particularly like, first finish that, especially if it is a more or less independent topic.

18. Don't count the number of pages left. Just work.

19. Reviewing what you have done every hour and a half or so will help it settle in your mind. Going through whatever you have done with someone else is also a great idea.

20. Don't count the number of pages left. Just work.

21. Take a fifteen-minute break every two hours or so and stretch. Take a walk. Do something you like which can be done quickly. I used to play the piano for a bit.

22. For me, I found writing stuff out twice or thrice made it mine and very easy to grasp and settled it in my mind.

23. Subjects can be Do subjects or Read subjects. If your subject involves doing, Do it. Maths and physics are Do subjects. You cannot 'do' history though. That you will just need to read and re-read. Don't make the mistake of trying to Read a Do subject.

24. If diagrams are involved, draw them a few times roughly. More importantly, label them.

25. Did I mention 'Don't count the number of pages left?' Just work!

From two hours before the exam, don't try to learn anything new. A review of everything you have managed to do once or twice is enough. Half an hour before the exam, completely stop studying and just relax. If nothing else, it unnerves everyone else around you.

Before taking the exam, drink some water and go to the toilet.

When you get the question paper, don't be in too much of a hurry to start answering it. First, say a quick prayer. You need help from everywhere!

Next, skim through the question paper. Identify the stuff you know or think you know and attempt that first. You don't have to answer the paper sequentially. Finish off stuff you are comfortable with, and then move on to the more challenging parts. It is also better to finish off the shorter answers first and to then attempt the longer ones.

Use a rough sheet for scribbling, or doing calculations. On your main answer sheet, write legibly and clearly. Preferably, underline or highlight key parts of your answer. Be neat.

Adding clearly labelled diagrams wherever applicable or a flow chart to your answers will help the examiner quickly realize you know your subject and possibly encourage them to give more credit.

There may be times when something that you are sure you know just refuses to come to mind during the exam. Or you get stuck at some step in the answer and simply can't remember what comes next. Don't despair. Leave that part blank and go to some other question. Come back to it after some time and you may be pleasantly surprised.

Attempt everything. Even if you know hardly anything about the question, write out whatever you do know. You may get lucky and get some credit for it.

The last ten minutes should ideally be spent going over your answer sheet and tidying it up. But if you are running late and need to finish off an answer, do that. It's always better to have an extra answer done rather than have a few lines drawn to make things look neater.

Once you are done, turn in your answer sheet and leave. Don't bother with discussing the questions and their probable answers with others. What you have written, you have written; there is nothing you can do about it and your grades will come to you sooner or later. You have other exams to get through.

Go home. Drink water or juice or eat something light and rest ... and then, get ready for the next round!

SECRETS OF STUDYING EFFECTIVELY

'I can't study this. I just can't.'

This is such a disempowered statement. And totally untrue. What do you mean, you can't study? Of course you can. But you didn't, or don't.

This distinction makes a huge difference.

Saying, 'I cannot do' something means that there is a physical or mental limitation preventing you from doing it. Saying, 'I didn't do' something means you could have, but chose not to. And when you could have done it but didn't, then you can now choose to do it and well ... do it!

Taking responsibility for your actions and inactions helps you dramatically increase the chances of success in life.

No one is born with a pathological hatred of a subject hardwired into his or her DNA. You develop this because of circumstances. At some point of time, you choose not to like a particular subject. Most often this is because the teacher who is teaching it sucks, and you are too naïve to hate the teacher. So you transfer the hatred of the teacher to the subject.

And go through life moaning about how you hate maths or physics or whatever. Hate the teacher if you have to. Don't hate the subject. Consciously choose to like it and you will be surprised at the proficiency you develop in it.

To start with, know that you CAN do it. If for any reason you have not done it so far, it doesn't matter. Start with, I can do this, and I *will* do it!

Once this bit is out of the way, a few questions need to be answered.

When should I start?

A good time is right now!

Just before you start work, I would heartily recommend that you do one or both of the focusing techniques described in Chapter 22. Do them once a day, every day, and over time you will be surprised how easy it becomes for you to focus on the work at hand. The few minutes spent in practicing these focus techniques will give your concentration levels a solid boost.

It's best to do these practices just before you start your work.

Should I have a timetable?

Quick answer: No.

You will waste precious time making it, and then 99 per cent of the time you will not follow it. Next you will feel bad and guilty for not sticking to it. Then you will get depressed, frustrated and angry and spend even more time making another timetable. And so on.

As long as you have some idea of what you are going to start with and what you will end with and approximately how long it will take, you are good to go. A very little bit of time (an hour or so) spent in planning and creating a very amorphous structure may be time well spent.

Remember that planning out the how, what and when of studying is not going to get you knowledge of your subject or your grades. Actually, it is the studying that does that. So it's a great idea to actually study rather than waste time *planning* to study.

What should I start with?

This is the first question I used to ask myself when I would start prepping for an upcoming exam. The answer turned out to be pretty simple. Start with the stuff you like.

Choose the subjects that you are good at or the chapters in various subjects that you feel comfortable with, and get those done. Don't make the mistake that I used to make, which was start with the tough stuff and leave the good stuff to do later. The tough stuff just makes you depressed and takes away your confidence.

Worse, when time starts to run out, you may botch up the good stuff and end up in the exam hall in a supremely dejected state.

Before diving into a subject, a quick read of the entire syllabus is a great idea. Go through all the relevant textbooks and all your notes. This is just a cursory reading. You are simply getting to know what you are in for. Once you have a bird's-eye view of the scope of what you are going to be studying, then it is time to get into the details.

Most subjects you will study can be broken up into two areas. The basics are the fundamentals that you simply have to know. A thorough understanding of the fundamentals will allow you to tackle the more advanced concepts and applications. Spend time on getting the basics done. Don't rush into the more complicated stuff without prepping yourself in the basics. This will almost always lead to disaster.

So, to reiterate – start with the stuff you like (or think you do) and spend a decent amount of time getting the basics into your head. Then move on to the more challenging parts of what you need to finish.

Do Subjects and Read Subjects

There are basically two types of study material. The first is the Do type: mathematics, physics, chemistry, accounting, etc. Here you need to understand the basics and practise them by doing. This means solving problems, drawing diagrams, learning how one concept leads to the next, writing stuff out, all of it. If you have understood your material, there will not be a strain on your memory. Speed can matter a lot in these subjects and so regular consistent practice is what is really required.

The second are the Read type subjects: the languages, history, geography, psychology, etc., where you will need to organize and prioritize information to remember it. Learning these subjects will require a pretty good memory and an ability to express yourself by writing. You will need to get a good head start when studying these types of subjects, otherwise you may find yourself overwhelmed.

Some of what you will study will fall in between these two. You will need to remember facts and figures and have the ability to solve problems based on them.

Figuring out what type of material you are going to be studying right at the start will help you choose your strategy to tackle it. Memory-intensive material will require frequent revision and can be done anywhere. You can take your notes and books to a park and work there, for example. Intelligence-intensive material will require lots of practice and will usually require a more formal study environment.

Should I study by myself or in a group?

If possible, you need to do a mix of both.

Decide on who are going to be your study partners. I would not recommend a circle of more than three or four people. Most times just two people work really great. Make sure these are people you like and who like you. You are going to be interdependent on each other. All of you should aim for collective victory and feel genuinely happy for each other's success. Make sure all of you understand what each of you is going to be doing.

In the first phase, study independently; this is when all of you need to get the basics done. Grasp all the fundamentals and get them firmly into your head. Then revise the basics with your group so that everyone is more or less on the same page. If any of you need help in this phase, make sure they get it. If they are making up excuses for not having completed their work, maybe you need to move away from them. They may become parasites in the long run.

In the next phase, go through the syllabus collectively and decide which topics each of you will master. These are topics that could be fairly independent of each other. Finish studying these by yourselves and then take turns in the group sessions to teach everyone what you have learnt. Constantly challenge yourself and your partners by asking questions so that each and every one of you is clear about everything.

Teaching others what you know will crystallize that aspect of the subject for you and help others learn it with very little effort. It is a fantastic win-win.

You will see that when a group of closely-knit people work like this, it takes considerably less effort for everyone to learn much faster. This type of studying also prepares you for later life because it teaches you the very valuable lessons of collaboration and the effectiveness of collective effort to achieve a target. Best of all, everyone comes out a winner.

When you are moving together, if one falls behind, the others pull them along. There is a greatly reduced chance of failure. There is a danger, however, and it is that during the group study sessions you end up talking about life, the universe and every type of inconsequential philosophical gossip and never get down to doing meaningful work. A bit of time-pass talking is fine, but too much of it can destroy all in the group. However, over the years, I have seen that this is a risk worth taking because of the tremendous benefits it brings to everyone involved.

Do have fun studying with each other. Crack jokes and laugh. The naughtier, the better, especially if they relate to the subject matter on hand. But don't make the mistake of doing only that. After a group study session, everyone should feel they have learnt something and moved a few steps closer to mastering the subject.

When a study circle works well, it is almost miraculous how much can get done!

Even if you choose to study completely by yourself, take some time off and teach what you have learnt to some other people. Teaching greatly helps clarification and retention. Others will also appreciate your gesture!

Where should I study?

You can study anywhere, especially if it is a Read subject. Go wherever you want and work. Choose a place where there will be minimal distraction and disturbance for optimum use of your time.

Having said that, a fixed place to study, with your computer, books, stationery and whatever else you require to work close at hand, is always a great idea. Preferably, this place should be well-ventilated and well-lit. Research has found that temperature-between 23-26 °Celsius are best for your brain cells to perform. If this is not possible where you are, a good library is a fantastic place to go to.

For group study, a room where all of you can be comfortable and where good munchies are at hand is great.

Keeping only the material you require for tackling the subject nearby and moving other stuff out of the way is a great idea.

Your brain can pick up subliminal cues from the environment that you study in. It could be a good idea to study in different places as well so that your learning becomes location independent.

Some people need music playing while studying. Others simply can't do any work without a TV blasting somewhere. I had gone once through a phase where I would blast ABBA at top volume when I was working. It helped me focus somehow and simultaneously broadcasted to the entire neighbourhood that I was studying. Sometime after, a neighbour was ill and they requested me to keep the volume of the music at a minimum. Soft music somehow irritated me, so I shut the music off completely and in about a fortnight or so got used to studying without it. I was quite taken aback at how much more efficient I had become.

If your exams are fast approaching, don't try changing any habit you have formed. If not, studying in a quiet place almost always works better once you get used to it.

How long should I study?

I don't like this question. I have never given much importance to how long anyone has studied. That really doesn't matter. What matters is how much of whatever you are doing has taken up residence in your head.

Some people work for about an hour and then get saturated. Others can plug on easily for 4-5 hours, sometimes even longer.

More than 90 per cent of processing and wrestling with a challenge is done by your subconscious while your mind is away from that particular problem. If you constantly attack a problem without giving yourself rest, you don't give your subconscious a chance to wrangle with it and the solution will elude you. Your subconscious registers problems and challenges and works on them while you are doing other things. Giving it a bit of time to grapple with tough things is always a great idea. A hot, relaxing shower or a scoop of chocolate ice cream does wonders for me!

I would recommend working at a stretch for about an hour at a time. While working, there will come a time when you start to feel saturated. If you start to feel tired and saturated before an hour is up, then you need to discipline yourself and see to it that you are working non-stop for at least an hour. Start with at least 20 minutes of focused study and gradually build it up to at least an hour, if not more.

If saturation happens after an hour or more of work, stop and take a break. Your break time should not be more than twenty minutes. Go for a short walk, munch on something, play the guitar, sing, meditate … Do whatever you want to that takes you away from your desk. Don't check your email or chat on Facebook, however.

Then come back and start again. Many times, you may be pleasantly surprised with sudden understanding of something you have been wrestling with, or a flash of inspiration to solve a stubborn problem. This is your subconscious at work.

If you look at the greatest inventions and discoveries, you will see there is a pattern to them. A vision, a dream, or a happening catalyses the solution. Stories talk about an apple falling on Newton's head and him coming up with the concept of gravity. Kekule dreams about three snakes eating each other and comes up with the benzene ring structure; and everyone knows about Archimedes in his bathtub…

Solutions to big problems have almost always happened through some sort of mistake or accident. These solutions seem to come when after furious mental activity, the person concerned, relaxes for a bit.

This is the anatomy of inspiration. Work hard at a problem to the point of absolute saturation and then let go. Do something that relaxes you, and nine times out of ten, the solution will come to you. Give your subconscious a chance to work for you. If you know how to meditate, do that at least twice a day. If you have not learnt how to meditate, take some time out and learn. It will give you an almost unfair advantage over people who don't meditate.

Work for an hour or more, to the point of saturation. Take a twenty-minute break. Get away from your books, your desk and your computer. Do something relaxing, something you thoroughly enjoy. Come back and work. You can go on for a very long time like this.

Remember to do some physical exercise every day, preferably every few hours – some stretches, a few surya namaskars or some walking will greatly freshen you up. Splashing cold water on your face and rinsing out your eyes with it feels absolutely wonderful and will enliven you.

It's a great idea to intertwine the study of two to three subjects or two to three different parts of a particular subject during your various study sessions in a day. This gives time for one to settle in the subconscious while you are consciously tackling another. You will be surprised at how stuff you learn in one subject can become super relevant for understanding stuff in another. For example, the concept of a derivative in math is the same as the concept of speed in physics.

Perhaps most importantly, you will *have* to evolve your methodology for studying as you progress in academia. What worked for you up to Grade 12 will definitely not work for you in graduate school and beyond. You will require different approaches and strategies. All the things we talk about in this book will allow you to form these for yourself and excel at your work.

Almost nothing beats the quiet satisfaction you get from cracking a concept or finally being able to understand something that's been eluding you. The high of solving a tough problem or figuring out a simpler, cleaner way of doing it and then teaching it to friends is quite unbeatable!

USING THE BRAIN

Everyone knows that we learn through our brain. I had been often told by teachers and parents to 'use my brains'. No one told me exactly how to do that though, or how learning actually happens in the brain.

There are libraries of books written by people who have dedicated their lives to the workings of the brain, and mostly, it is only those people who understand them. For folks like you and me, a few basics of what makes the brain tick are enough to … well, use our brains.

The adult human brain weighs about 1,400 gms. A liquid called the cerebrospinal fluid (CSF) surrounds the brain, running all the way down our spinal cord as well. And so the brain actually floats in our skull and has a net weight of just twenty-five grams! This is great news because if the CSF was not there, or if the brain was much heavier, its own weight would cut off the blood supply from it, and we wouldn't last very long. The entire assembly of the skull rests on just two really small vertebrae – the atlas and the axis, which would never be able to hold the actual weight of the brain along with all the surrounding paraphernalia. We would literally loose our head. It would simply fall off. Nature has cleverly injected just that 125 ml or so of CSF into our systems so that those niggling problems could be resolved.

The brain consists of three major parts – the cerebrum, the cerebellum and the brain stem. The cerebrum is the largest part of the brain and it is associated with higher brain functions like thought and (voluntary) action. The cerebellum receives information from the senses and coordinates voluntary movements such as posture, balance, coordination and speech, resulting in smooth and balanced muscular activity. The brain stem is involved in regulating the basic functions, like heart rate, breathing, sleeping and eating.

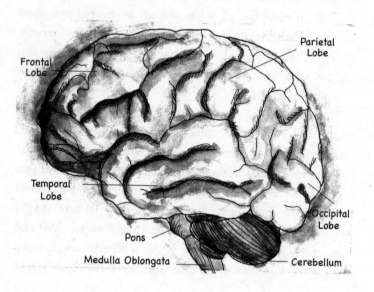

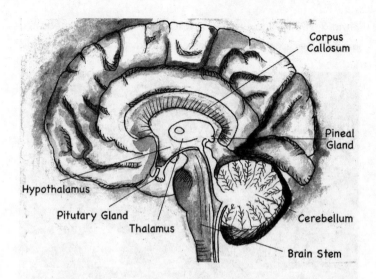

The brain has a dense network of fibre pathways that contains a humongous number of neurons – approximately 100 billion of them! Our brain is incredibly plastic. What this means is that whenever we learn something new, we actually change the wiring of our brain on a deep level, as we shall see in this chapter.

Whenever you listen, see, talk, read, write, feel, taste or practise something, fibres called dendrites grow out of the neurons. New dendrites take time to grow. When two dendrites grow close together, a connection is formed between them. This is called a synapse. Messages travel along these synapses from one neuron to another as electrical signals.

As learning happens, specific dendrites need to grow and connect to other specific dendrites along specific synapses. There can be up to 10,000 synapses per neuron, of which there are around 100 billion. This can lead to some fairly complicated maths ... we may need to grow some dendrites to process all this!

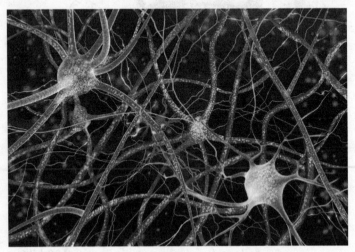

Artist's impression of the brain under a microscope.

Some synapses are weak, while others are strong. Some are so weak that they don't send a signal (forgetting). Learning is the process of making weak synapses strong. As you practise doing something, the dendrites grow thicker (imagine the speed of data transfer going from 2G to 3G and then to 4G and above) with a fatty covering called myelin. As the dendrites grow thicker, information travels faster and with less interference. (You can easily focus and concentrate on things you have practised, and other stuff happening around you doesn't bother you.) With more practice, your dendrites figure out that this is important for you and actually make a double connection. This ensures that you remember what you have learnt for a very long time. Practice makes the connections stronger and stronger, so be sure to practise very carefully.

I remember when I was learning to play the piano, I thought I would surprise my teacher by learning a new part of a sonata I was studying by myself. I practised the entire week before class, so I could get it right for her. Unfortunately I had got a few notes wrong, but my wrong practice had wired it so firmly into my brain that I had to actually drop that piece and start with another. I never managed to learn that particular sonata and have had to content myself with hearing other people play it.

When you learn something new, the dendrites are very small and fragile and can vanish pretty quickly. seventy per cent of anything new is forgotten within twenty-four hours if it is not practised right away. However, if you practise whatever new stuff you have learnt within twenty-four hours, and then, a bit later practise it again, you keep 80 per cent or more!

It is interesting to note that simply practising what you have learnt many, many times on the same day you learnt it doesn't strengthen the neural pathways quite as much as practising the same thing once or twice a day over the next week to ten days, possibly giving gaps of a day or two before coming back to it.

For example, if you learnt something new on Monday, go back to it on Tuesday, Wednesday, Friday and Sunday. Don't touch it on Thursday and Saturday. This is far better than going through it again and again on Monday itself.

When I say practise here, I don't mean simply reading or writing the material again and again. You need to be able to recall it. So keep that book around you shut and see how much you can recall of whatever it is that you want to learn. In other words, practise recall. This gets the bunch of dendrites that have been formed for that particular material to learn to fire together, efficiently and smoothly. It also helps these bits of material to 'link' to other bits of material, so you keep getting a better idea of the bigger picture. This is where mind mapping becomes an utterly invaluable tool. A chapter on mind mapping coming up next.

It may be a good idea to change your study environment. You get subliminal cues from your environment when you are working and your neurons become more 'comfortable' to fire in that environment. The place you are going to give your exam, or sit for that interview, could be very different from the place you study and you might experience sluggish neural activity. Therefore, when you are practising recall, see if you can do it in different environments so that your neuron firing becomes location independent.

Forgetting is actually good for you, according to new research. When your brain retrieves a half-forgotten memory, it is working very hard and so when you review your work, you are making very strong connections. So don't be bothered that you have forgotten a lot of what you studied. The dendrites are right there ... some connections have faded, but when they come back on, they will be much, much stronger.

You grow dendrites for exactly what you are doing. If you watch physics problems being solved, you will grow dendrites to watch them getting solved. If you actually solve the problems yourself, you will grow dendrites to solve the problems. Big difference!

Be careful of 'bad' habits. Watching too much TV, for example, can cause too many of those dendrites to grow, giving your brain the wrong signal that this is very important for you.

Interestingly, emotions play a huge role in the learning process. Strong emotions make strong memories.

If you are feeling scared or anxious, adrenaline courses through your body and this inhibits the neurons from transmitting information (forgetting stuff during an exam). If you are feeling safe, relaxed and happy, endorphins are secreted and this allows you to recall better and also make new connections as you solve stuff that comes up in your life. Meditation makes you feel relaxed and quietly confident. No wonder then that people who meditate have such a huge edge over people who don't! Their brain chemistry is altered by meditation, making their brain vastly superior for learning and remembering.

Our brains are naturally programmed to seek out and remember new and unusual things. If something happens that is mundane, the brain compares it with memories that already exist and if things match, then it is considered redundant and discarded. If something new happens, the brain goes into a frenzy trying to match it with stuff it has already experienced and if it doesn't, AND it deems it important, then this experience is stored as a memory.

A significant factor that contributes to the growth of dendrites is how many of our senses are involved in the learning process. According to studies, we remember:

10 per cent of what we read
20 per cent of what we hear
30 per cent of what we see
50 per cent of what we see and hear
70 per cent of what is discussed with others
80 per cent of what we experience ourselves and
a staggering 95 per cent of what we teach to someone else!

To learn, you need to be interested. You need to get excited about it. Don't worry if it is something new. Something new simply means you need to grow some dendrites and your brain is perfectly capable of doing that. Once you are interested in something, you automatically discuss this with others. You try and see if you can experience it for yourself. A new worthwhile experience is a guaranteed long-term memory!

Once you have learnt it well, you teach it to others. They thank you for it, you feel great about yourself, and most importantly, that bit of knowledge is now pretty much wired into your system. You are not going to forget it in a hurry.

Finally, taking a break after working hard at something helps strengthen connections and make new connections. Flashes of insight come when you rest after a substantial amount of study. This is not restricted to just studying. It is for any activity. If you have been practising really hard at basketball, for instance; take a day off and come back to the game and you will be surprised at the skill you have suddenly acquired.

As we saw in an earlier chapter, sleep plays a supremely important part for the healthy functioning of our brain. When you are sleeping, your brain is performing some very crucial functions. Not only is it clearing out the brain poo that has accumulated because of the mental activity during the day, it is also strengthening stuff you want to remember and erasing stuff you don't. Amazingly, it also rehearses things that you are finding difficult to grasp.

A good night's sleep doesn't just make you fresher. It makes you smarter as well!

Learning is just a matter of growing dendrites and strengthening the connections between them. Summarizing factors that influence stronger connections and better learning –

1. More of your senses are involved in the learning process.
2. Practising what you have learnt within twenty-four hours of learning it and then a few times again within a week. Make sure you are practising correctly. Practise makes perfect, but wrong practise can make you perfectly wrong! While practising, make sure you practise the tough stuff too, not just what you find easy. Give yourself quick tests to see if you really remember so that you don't fool yourself into thinking you know the material.
3. Revisiting new material over a week to ten days, giving gaps of a day or two in between, will strengthen those neural pathways, making that material truly yours. When you revisit, remember to practise recall, rather than just read or write from your notes or the textbook. Preferably do it in different environments so that your knowledge becomes location independent.
4. Forgetting is all right. When you get back to your work and start to remember stuff, the connections the dendrites make are much stronger.
5. You grow dendrites for exactly what you are doing. So be aware of what you are doing. You are growing dendrites that will wire themselves deep within your brain. Make sure you want them.
6. Emotions play a big role in strengthening memories. When you are stressed, adrenaline flows. This inhibits your neurons from firing correctly. When relaxed, endorphins are secreted. Your neurons love being relaxed and calm. Meditation will grant you a HUGE edge towards success in life.
7. New things that are perceived as relevant turn on our brains.

8. Discussing and teaching what you have learnt will allow you to retain 95 per cent and above with yourself, besides making you quite popular as well.
9. After substantial practice, taking a break will miraculously make it more natural and easy. You may even get flashes of insight as dendrites make new connections.
10. Do remember to sleep your seven to nine hours every night. It allows your brain to detox, reinforces stuff you need to remember, deletes irrelevant things and rehearses tough material you are learning.

When you have understood how the brain works and that the learning that happens through practice, discussion, feeling great about yourself and teaching what you have learnt to others is going to be with you for a very long time ... that next exam is going to be a piece of cake!

MIND MAPPING AND
RADIAL THINKING

If you have read the chapter on using your brain and seen the picture of the neurons, you will agree that it seems to be a big wonderful, enchanting, chaotic mess in there. Definitely not a neat and orderly list!

One of the biggest impediments to learning and recall is sequential thinking. It's a bad habit that society and families impose upon us – doing and thinking about only one thing at a time. Forcing us into patterns of linear thinking. Making lists, and then ticking off stuff one thing at a time until we are through. Making more lists. Rinse and repeat. It's borrrrrrringggg!

Linear thinking makes learning into drudgery, and recall becomes wishful thinking. Most of us barely remember what we studied, say in the first year of engineering, when we get to the third year. All we want to do is stop the learning and the studying and get on with real life…

This is chiefly because we are not using our brain the way it was meant to be. The earlier chapter granted many insights on exactly how to do that. This chapter is about a technique that accomplishes precisely this. It's called mind mapping. A British psychology author, Tony Buzan, has even laid claim to having originated mind maps, though people have been making such drawings for years.

It's just a few circles and lines really. Underneath its simplicity, however, there is a vast amount of science that we will not go into over here (thankfully). It's a profoundly easy way to use the brain how it's meant to be used, and I would really recommend that you do a formal course on learning how to mind map … But till then, this chapter will do to get you off and running with mind maps.

Unlike most other chapters in this book, this is not a 'read' chapter. It's a 'do' chapter. Remember that actually drawing the mind maps is going to grow the 'drawing' mind map dendrites in your brain. Just reading and looking at the pictures will grow the wrong dendrites and won't bring you the proficiency you require to use this technique effectively.

Before moving on with this chapter, make sure you have the following things at hand:

1. A few pencils and pens of different colours. Red, blue, black and green pens and a box of Crayola work perfectly.
2. A ruler and an eraser.
3. Plenty of A4-sized blank sheets of paper, preferably without the ruling.
4. A few white chart papers.
5. If you are feeling artistic, get more colours, felt pens, etc.

When you turn the page, you will have some exercises to do. It will take you less than forty-five minutes to complete them. Please do them in the order they are given. By the end of these exercises, you will have learnt the point and the basics of mind mapping.

The Party

Say you are throwing a party for some dear friends that you have not met in a while. They all happen to be in the same city you are and have called and asked to be entertained at your home (they were clear they didn't want to go out). A small intimate party with very good friends is the idea.

Make a list of what you would require to make the party a super success. Make it as exhaustive as possible. Do this with a paper and pen, not on an electronic device.

Start with their names. Name two or three people you know who are dear to you and you have not met in a long time. Now, customize the party for them. What are they going to eat? How is the house going to look? What's the entertainment going to be like? Plan the entire evening out. Take ten or fifteen minutes to do this. You may take longer if you wish.

Don't turn the page until you are ready with your plan.

A To Do List

Start on another list. Make a list of things you need to do tomorrow. This list has nothing to do with your party list. Take at least five or ten minutes. Once you are ready, read on.

Take a few more minutes and see if you wish to add anything else to either of your two lists. Take your time on this. Once you have got both your lists more or less finalized, read on.

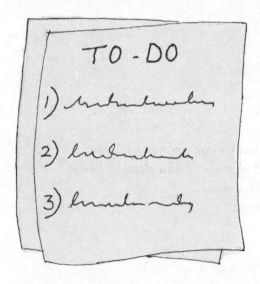

On the next few pages are plans for three very different parties and three things to do tomorrow lists. Go through them. If you feel you want to add anything from these lists to any of yours, please do so. Any more ideas you may get for either of your lists should be added in now. Take some time over this.

Party I:

Kapil Mathur.
Bhavesh Shah.
Nimesh Sangrachka.
Make sure everyone knows the way to my house. Google Map them the directions.
Clean up the house.
Have lots of candles all over the place. This makes it cosy and intimate.

Menu:

Dhokla.
Khandvi.
Handvo.
Green Chutney (not too spicy).
Fruit and veggie salad with plenty of greens.
Dressing for salad.
Shahi Paneer.
Biryani.
Raita.
Dry Mixed Veggies.
Rotis.
Gulab Jamun.
Chocolate ice cream with nuts.

Have some time to meditate with Sri Sri's meditation CD.

Make playlists of Garba, old Hindi film songs, Andrew Lloyd Webber.

Board game – Mumbai Connection on hand, also pack of cards.

Gifts: Make custom T-shirts for each of them with some crazy captions.

Party II:

Shweta Vyas.
Puja Handa.
Rita Billimoria.
Clean up the house, decorate with flowers, put away expensive stuff and make the house baby friendly (Puja just had a baby).
Make rangoli outside house.
Tea lights in places baby cannot get to.
Personal: A trip to the beauty parlour, waxing, pedicure, manicure, hair spa – the works!
Baby pink salwar (with embroidery).
Gold chain with Devi pendant.
Diamond studs.
Gold and ruby bangles.
Practice all the Hindi film songs we know on guitar, they will want to sing.

Menu:

Fruit juices and mocktails.
Lots of finger food – pakoda, Bhajia, Dhokla, Batatavada with chutney.
Mushroom soup with bread and garlic-herbed butter.
Pani puri and chaat.

Paneer Tikka (make sure lime slices are there to squeeze on paneer).
Veggie Pulao.
Pineapple Raita.
Malai Kofta.
Rotis.
Warm gooey chocolate cake.

Keep toothpicks and paper towels handy.
Set the dining table in the garden; chairs, plates and cutlery; decorate with fairy lights.
Old photos, ABBA and Carpenters music, *Mamma Mia* and *Hum Aapke Hain Koun.!* movies … Not too much of this, will want to talk, talk, and talk …
Gift embroidered towels to all of them. Have to get names embroidered from Tulips.

Party III

Lalit.
Jogi.
Abhay.
All of them are foodies and super chefs, so will have them help in making food. Most of the party will be in the kitchen. Everything needs to be prepped and ready.

Expand Kitchen!

Get another oven and an induction stove from Mona.
Get an induction stove from Krishna.

Keep Monin syrups – vanilla, green apple, grenadine, mango.
Margarita glasses and salt spread on plate.
Sprite.
Lemon.
Fresh mint and basil leaves.
Spaghetti cooked to al dente.
Cheeses – cheddar, parmesan, fresh mozzarella, gorgonzola,
gouda.
Thirty tomatoes, peeled.
Garlic bread.
Paneer at room temperature.
Broccoli cut into florets.
Mushrooms – button, oyster, shiitake – washed and dried.
Green peas, shelled and parboiled.
Lettuce. Rocket leaves.
Baby spinach.
Avocado.
Sundried tomatoes.
Extra virgin olive oil.
Organic honey.
Dessert will be panna cotta that I will make along with a
strawberry dressing.
Soft music, anything really, as long as it is non-intrusive.
We will cook to our hearts' content and eat till our stomachs
burst!
Make arrangements for sleep over for everyone, after such a
meal they won't want to go back. New shorts and T-shirts for all
three. Blankets and sheets.
  If they are staying over, keep movies and board games
handy.

Get Mumbai Connection out and Cirque du Soliel blu-rays.
Hot chocolate in the night.

To Do I:

Sadhana:
    12 surya namaskars with mantras.
    Sudarshan Kriya.
    Padmasadhana (with Sahaj).
    Listen to Devi kavacham.
    Read Geeta few pages.
Sort out videos for editing for my YouTube channel (BnDtv).
Make sure to feed the dogs.
Watch Bahubali fight scene.
Water the plants.
Finish cleaning kitchen for Deepawali.
Decide photographer's website template for Tanna.
Go to Uppi's house for lunch; remember to take jam for aunty.
Bank reconciliation statement for the month.

To Do II:

Exercise: Warm up and shoulders.
Chant Gayatri Mantra.
Dentist appointment.
Emails and Facebook.
Finish building the restaurant website for client.
Dance class in the evening, practise during day if possible.
Book tickets while sale is on for Delhi.
Meeting with team for marketing strategy, especially during festival time.

Dad's birthday present, James Bond set, find Region A and order it.

Migrate to new phone.

To Do III:

Breakfast for everyone.

Cereals with milk.

Orange juice.

Tea.

Coffee.

Chop up papaya.

Lunch for kids.

Rotis.

Rajma and rice.

Cauliflower and potatoes veggie.

Gulab jamun.

Meditate!

Sort out my wardrobe.

Get the maids to clean the fans and vacuum the curtains.

Meeting with all moms in building for making compost out of kitchen waste.

Take Bhuvana to violin class.

Take Aarman to volleyball match.

Beauty parlour at 3 p.m. for pedicure and hair spa (?)

Yoga class.

Finish emails.

Plan for vacation coming next month.

Make sure some homework with kids is done.

Dinner:
Spaghetti in red sauce with garlic bread (get the bread from Vishala).
Clear soup.
Hot chocolate just before bed (get powder from store, we are running out).

As you read through all the lists above, you will surely get ideas for your two lists. Go ahead and add them in. Don't worry about being neat or anything like that. Make sure you capture all the ideas that pop into your head. You may want to go over the six lists above two or three more times. Turn the page when you are ready.

See my original lists shown in Illustration 1 and 3. Whereas, Illustrations 2 and 4 are the same lists on which I added many other thoughts and ideas that I got as I went through others' lists and party plans and thought about everything a bit more.

There were so many great ideas I found that I wanted to add them into mine as well. As I added them in, my pages became quite a mess. If I had used the blue pen, it would have looked even messier. If you followed the exercise, I bet your plans look quite messy as well!

Did you notice how difficult it was to add new ideas?

Look at this artist's impression of the wonderful mess of neurons and neural pathways in your brain.

Which one resembles the way your brain is wired?

Which one is easier to look at?

Do you see how easy it would be to add an idea to this mind map?

Just a line and a circle and voila, we are done.

It gives a bird's-eye view and a worm's-eye view at the same time. I can see the whole and really get into details if I wish to, at any node.

Did you notice that even though you had the freedom to add ideas to either the party plan or the things to do tomorrow list, you kind of stuck to just one of them, even though ideas for the other were popping into your head? This is the conditioning of 'doing one thing at a time', or sequential thinking.

Wouldn't you agree that adding ideas to both mind maps at any time, jumping from one idea to another and back again, would make your thinking more organic and natural? Mind maps allow you to do this with consummate ease.

Welcome to the world of radial thinking!

Thinking radially, and allowing ideas to flow naturally rather than inhibiting them makes the process of learning and recall much easier.

The 0-1-2-3 of mind mapping:

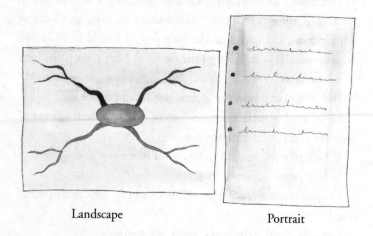

Landscape

Portrait

Take a blank sheet of paper and turn it sideways – landscape style. It's quite amazing to note that when you keep it in portrait style, your brain finds it easier to go into 'list' mode. When you look at it in landscape mode, your brain goes into 'radial' mode.

1. Start with a central idea. You may want to give some thought to exactly what your central idea should be for a particular mind map. For example, if you had to mind map *Romeo and Juliet*, what would you make your central idea? 'Tragedy' or 'Love Story' or something else? As you can imagine, the resulting mind maps for the two different ideas would be

quite different. The central idea gives a perspective to the project you are going to be mind mapping.

2. Draw four or five lines radiating out from the central idea and jot down whatever ideas come to you as you draw them related to the central idea. Don't worry about how important or relevant your ideas are.

3. See if more ideas flow from the various nodes you just created.

Rinse and repeat!

This makes mind mapping a very powerful tool for ideation.

You have a task – write an essay about butterflies.

Here is how I would start.

Put the central idea as 'Butterfly Business'.

Egg, caterpillar, pupa and adult were the four ideas that jumped at me right away. (See Illustration 5)

Once I had those down, I started reading up a bit about butterflies from the net and as I read a few articles, those four nodes got developed as shown in this mind map. (See Illustration 6)

As I continued my research, I found a very cool little piece about how butterflies mate, so I made that into a node all by itself. The internet is peppered with many fascinating facts about these beautiful creatures and that became another node. After that it was just populating these nodes with information. I ended up with my final mind map. I showed it to Deepa, an artist friend of mine, and she came up with this! (See Illustrations 7.)

From the mind map and my research on the net, I wrote this piece.

Butterfly Business

Butterflies use visual clues and/or complex chemicals called pheromones to find their mates. Mating happens in the air or on the ground, and the male transfers a sperm packet called a spermatophore into the female.

Internal fertilization can take from a few seconds to a few hours, depending on the species of the butterfly. The female will then lay an egg or clusters of eggs on a host plant that she considers to be appropriate. Most eggs are attached with a fast-drying glue-like chemical that the female secretes while laying the eggs.

Various different species lay eggs in various different places – the underside of leaves, flower heads and the crevices in tree bark are common places. One type of butterfly called the ghost moth actually lays thousands of eggs while flying. The larva of this species eats grass.

The eggs come in various shapes and colours. They could be spherical, oval or pod-shaped and green, white or yellow in colour. The eggs have a thin, tough shell and are ribbed. These ribs are called reticulations. They have a tiny pit called the micropyle which marks the place the sperm has entered the egg. Air and water enter the egg through the micropyle while the egg develops.

There is yolk inside each egg, which nourishes the larva while it develops. Once the larva is ready, it gnaws through the shell of the egg and emerges as a caterpillar who eats its egg as its first meal.

The caterpillar's job is simple. It eats. And eats. And eats. It constantly eats and grows at an astounding rate. This stage can last from two weeks to about a month. Their diet is pretty limited. Normally they will eat only the leaves of the plant that their mother carefully chose for them. Some are carnivores too; for example, the larvae of the harvester butterfly eat only woolly aphids.

As caterpillars grow, their exoskeleton becomes too tight for them, so they moult (lose their exoskeleton). After moulting, while their skin is still soft, they swallow a lot of air so that their bodies expand. After their new skin hardens, they let the air out, so they now have place to grow on the insides. Typically a caterpillar will moult four to five times.

When their growth is done, their phenomenal appetites sated, the larva stops eating and prepares to pupate. It will empty its digestive system and leave a small dark spot. Then it looks for a safe sheltered place to turn into a pupa.

Once it has found the place, it attaches itself with a silken girdle around its abdomen and a silken pad and cremaster (a hook or a set of hooks) at the hind part of its abdomen. It then splits open, loses its exoskeleton and becomes a pupa.

This is the stage in the butterfly's life cycle when it is encased in a chrysalis and undergoes metamorphosis. It doesn't eat anything during this time. This stage can last for a few weeks to overwinter. In many species, about a day before the adult butterfly is ready to emerge, the chrysalis becomes transparent.

The adult butterfly emerges from the chrysalis fully grown. When the adult emerges, its wings are wrinkled and deflated, but the abdomen is full of fluid. It pumps this fluid into the wings through veins to inflate them. Then it rests and lets the wings dry out.

Adults can only eat liquids, which they sip through a straw-like proboscis. They will sip nectar from flowers, liquids from rotting fruit, mushy bird dung or mineral rich water from puddles. Some sip pollen. Few sip rotting flesh and the harvester butterfly sips the bodily liquid of woolly aphids. Very few, like the great silk moth, don't eat at all and die within a week to ten days.

The life span of a butterfly can vary greatly – from a week to about a year. Facts about butterflies:

1. Butterflies taste with their feet.
2. They don't have mouths.
3. They need the sun to fly. They can't fly if it's too cold.
4. They can see the colours red, yellow and green.
5. Their wings are actually transparent. They have tiny scales that give them the colour visible to us as light refracts off them.
6. Their skeletons are outside their body.
7. Some species migrate long distances, up to 3,500 kms. They do this over three to four generations. How they manage this is still a mystery.

The 6 Cs of Mind Mapping

C1: Central Idea: We already talked about this one earlier. It will be pivotal when it comes to the perspective your mind map will take. It can be decided in advance, like I did for the butterflies, or it may be resolved in retrospect, if you are unclear about what the topic is going to be. For example, if you are using a mind map to take notes.

C2: Conciseness: Write briefly on the nodes and branches – just enough to capture the essence of the ideas.

C3: Craziness: Our brain loves the new and crazy. Make things as funny as you possibly can. You will remember it better.

C4: Curves: Use curves instead of straight lines. Our brains love curves. It makes things far more visually attractive, which makes things more interesting; this grows the relevant dendrites required for learning.

C5: Colours: This one is a no-brainer. Colours appeal to us. Unless you are a professional photographer. In which case you use a $5,000 camera to take out of focus, black and white photos and call them art.

Use some colour in your mind maps. Vary text sizes and alignments. You could even use particular colours for coding stuff. In my 'to do' mind maps, I use green for 'easy', yellow for 'doable but tough', orange for 'doable, but only with help' and red for 'I could really use a lot of help!'.

C6: Cartoons: Draw a few doodles here and there on your mind map. Instead of writing 'first aid' for example, a small red cross would convey the idea so much better. 'I can't draw' is a myth. Everyone can draw. Maybe they draw badly to start with, but that's all right. Start somewhere. Keep at it and those dendrites will grow over time and you will learn. Pictures and cartoons trigger emotion, and that strengthens memory.

Typically, you will not be able to create the final version of any mind map the first time you start making it. Start with a rough version. Get all the nodes and the details you want radiating off those nodes on paper. The next draft will be drawing it again, making sure everything is more or less in the places you want it to be. You may want to shift a main node under some other node, or create a new main node, etc. The final draft is for you to use colours and cartoons and make it as neat and pretty as possible. When you have done this, it's highly improbable that you will ever forget what you have mind mapped, and even if you do, a few glances at your mind map will bring everything back in just a few minutes!

Of course, you need not do all this for all the mind maps you make. For example, when it's a mind map about what you are going to do today, a simple rough mind map is more than enough. Otherwise you may end up doing only that – making a mind map and never getting to the actual work.

There is a very interesting side effect of using mind maps extensively. Mind maps bring obvious clarity to you about organizing yourself and creating road maps for the way ahead. They bring clarity in your ideation. Your ability to think about things radially and logically becomes a force to be reckoned with. This clarity is super contagious. In just a little while of using mind maps, as your dendrites start growing and making all the right connections, you will suddenly, almost magically find answers to other things that you may not even have mind mapped at all. Things that may have been on the back-burner for a long time may abruptly get resolved. Problems that may have perplexed you for some time get solved almost without effort. New challenges that may come up start resolving themselves in a very short time.

The biggest disadvantage of mind maps is that they only show you the way. They bring clarity to your plans and create actionable stuff for you to execute. They don't make the actual execution happen. A beautifully created mind map about losing weight will only show you how to lose weight – it will not make you actually lose weight. For that you have to follow the mind map and do (or not do) stuff that will actually make you lose weight.

I have found that mind maps lend themselves brilliantly for the subjective type of study material. They are not nearly as effective for linear type of work, such as math theorems or physics problems. A recipe is quite linear, and as a challenge, I made a mind map of a recipe to make an utterly delicious and fabulously easy rasam that Gowrishankar taught me. Here is the recipe and its mind map.

Gowri's Utterly Delicious Rasam

You will need:

10 curry leaves

2-3 red chillies, depending on how spicy you want it

2 tsps of jeera

2 tsps of mustard seeds

10 cloves of garlic, just slightly crushed

2 heaped tbs of rasam powder (a little more if you want it spicier), dissolved in two glasses of water

1 tsp turmeric powder

2-3 pinches of hing

1-inch cube of jaggery, grated (a little more if you want it slightly sweeter)

1 tsp sugar

12 medium-sized tomatoes, washed and peeled

A slightly-bigger-than-lemon-sized ball of tamarind

Ghee
Small bunch of coriander leaves for garnish
Salt to taste

Soak the ball of tamarind in a glass of hot water for half an hour. Squish it nicely with your fingers. Strain. Reserve the water.

Puree 8 tomatoes and roughly chop the others into big chunks.

In a heavy-bottomed vessel, heat the ghee till it melts.

Add red chillies, curry leaves, jeera and mustard seeds and let them splutter for a few seconds.

Add garlic and sauté till golden brown.

Add (the dissolved) rasam powder, turmeric powder, hing and tamarind water. Add pureed tomatoes and a litre or so of water.

Add chopped tomatoes, sugar and jaggery. Bring to boil. Simmer on low or medium heat for about thirty minutes till everything is well cooked.

Add salt to taste.

Garnish with freshly chopped coriander leaves.

Serve piping hot with freshly cooked rice. Top with some home-made ghee for a truly divine experience.

The mind map for the recipe is Illustration 8.

The colours used in this mind map are of particular note. They bring a sense of logic and sequence to the recipe.

Mind maps and their use are limited only by your imagination. Unfortunately, they are also limited by the amount you practise and use them as well. You will need to diligently mind map for a few months to start seeing real results. Fortunately, mind maps are such fun to create and work with that these months just zip by.

Just imagine: if you mind mapped ten chapters of some book you need to study, revision of your work would be so easy. You would need to look at just ten pages for almost complete recall. The use of mind maps will revolutionize the way you approach studying and exams.

Need to prepare for an interview or a speech? Mind map it out. You will be able to create fantastic presentations in a fraction of the time you would normally have spent. Stuck for ideas on how to handle that new project that's been thrust on you? Mind maps will generate ideas out of the blue for you.

You and your team need to brainstorm on something? Use mind maps to effortlessly take notes. Create a final version; send it off to everyone in the team. Recap in the next meeting will be super quick and all the things to be done by each person will be crystal clear!

Mind maps make you so efficient that you will finally have the time to do all those things you have always wanted to do but found no time for.

In Chapter 18 there are some essays and their mind maps to get you started. For a few of them, read the essays and draw mind maps about them and compare these with the mind maps I have drawn. For others, study the mind map, fire up Google and do some research and come up with an essay to match the mind map. Then compare your essays with the ones I have written.

Happy mind mapping!

TEAMDOM

There are quite a few people who only study during their years in an educational institution. During this time, they hardly take part in any extra-curricular activities. No music, no dramatics, no sports, no debating; no nothing other than their academic work.

These people may score good grades on their exams but they miss out on an integral part of formal education, which is learning to deal with other people. Almost no one ever works alone after graduating.

Learning to work in a team or lead a team, or simply knowing how to get along with various types of people are core life skills that an astonishing number of people have never bothered to develop.

These people find it extremely difficult to get a job, and if they actually manage to get one, they are very slow to rise up the corporate ladder. If they start up something on their own, they want to do everything by themselves and always complain that they cannot find good people to rely on and so can never expand their businesses. They are secretive and don't trust others. Their businesses have a high attrition rate because they lack the people skills they should have developed in their formative years.

Working in a team or leading a team is quite an art and develops only with practice, with lots of trial and error. A team almost always achieves much, much more than an individual ever can. However, there are many things that can go wrong, and a bad team can also sometimes paralyse or jeopardize the work on hand.

Being in a team is like living in civilized society.

If you live alone in a forest somewhere, you can do pretty much anything you like, any time you like. You are completely free.

As soon as even one more person is added to the mix, there will suddenly be roles and responsibilities that will take shape. One person sleeps, the other person watches; then the roles interchange. One person forages, the other person cooks and so on. The freedom that one enjoyed earlier is compromised, but it is replaced by an enhanced quality of life and greater safety and security for both of you. Add a few more people, and what is created is known as a family, which is just the social name for a team.

Add a few families together and you have a village. Add more and more, and you have towns and cities. As you transform from your wild existence in the jungle to a civilized existence in a city, you find that though your freedom has been compromised to a great extent, your quality of life has improved dramatically.

We rely on each other for many, many things. There is an entire chain of people who grow the food we eat. Another chain makes the clothes we wear. Yet another chain supplies electricity, yet others supply water ... and so on. We are utterly dependent on each other, and this, amazingly, frees each of us to live our lives the way we want to, provided we do it within the boundaries set by society. When people trespass these boundaries, they are punished and could possibly be banished from society (put in a jail) until they are ready to integrate.

If you wish to enjoy the quality of life that you do right now, you have to remember that you belong to a society. Many people may depend upon you to fulfil your role, just as you are dependent on them for fulfilling theirs.

This is basically what a team is, and how many teams together form organizations. Each is dependent on the other to make life easier for all and to be able to fulfil the overall goals that have been laid out for all. If you know how to live in society, you know how to work in a team. If you are a successful team player, you know all about relationships and families.

Just as you can never forget that you live in a city or are part of a family, the one overarching thing you should remember when you are part of a team is that you are part of a team!

Being a Team Player

There are many aspects to being a team player. Being a good communicator is important. Communicate honestly, lucidly and directly. Remain positive. Positivity brings energy to your words and ideas. Negativity will suck the vitality of the entire team. Share relevant information in meetings as well as informally with colleagues.

Definitely speak your mind, but if your ideas are not accepted, you still need to give your 100 per cent. That's part of being a team player. You need to respect the opinions of the rest of your team and your team leader's authority. If things work out well, you were part of a successful team, and if they don't, at least you get to say, 'I told you so!'

Know how to share news. If you have good news, share it with your colleagues. Rejoice in your success and the success of the team. This way the entire team will get inspired and propelled to achieving even loftier goals. Share with your superiors as well for well-earned recognition. Mainly, good news needs to flow around and downwards.

If you have bad news, share it only with your superiors, or with the people who can do something about it. Sharing bad news with colleagues who have no skill to deal with the issue can potentially create panic and transform a problem into a crisis. Keep bad news only flowing upwards.

Be flexible and open to change. Change is a given. Your response to change will determine if you and your team succeed.

I used to have two places where I would teach Art of Living courses. Two teams of around ten people each would volunteer their time and effort to organize these courses. Both teams were quite similar in terms of their qualifications, their backgrounds, their skill sets and how much time they could give for the work on hand. I, too, gave equal amounts of time to both the teams. Surprisingly, one of the teams consistently did much better than the other, and I couldn't figure out why.

When I gave it some thought, I realized they had one crucial advantage over the other. Once in a while in a meeting, I would give them a fairly challenging task. When faced with this, the team that used to perform well would immediately start brainstorming about how to handle the challenge, and the space would be full of positivity and ideas.

The other team would spend more than half the time trying to convince me why the task was not doable. They would take a very long time to accept that a particular thing needed to be done and meanwhile operate through minds full of denial or complaints. The simple act of accepting that something needs to be done can make work happen in so much more simpler and faster ways.

When faced with a task, come up with ideas on how to accomplish it. Don't waste time giving reasons about why it cannot be done. Accept that it has to happen and figure out ways of making it happen.

These simple things, when followed, will make you an effective team player. You will find yourself in great demand, just as I was.

Being a Team Leader:

Sooner or later you will get to lead a team of your own. A team leader can make or break a team. He could provide an exhilarating work environment, or he could break the team and make people feel weary, miserable, frustrated, confused and disheartened.

With. This single word can make such a huge difference in the way a leader leads a team.

One leader says he has a team working under him. Another says he has a team working *with* him!

A leader who works with his team will attract tremendous talent. They are able to hold on to and manage people who are far more skilled than themselves in their areas of expertise.

A person who has people work under him will always have sub-standard people who he can boss around or sycophants who will easily manipulate him. Intelligent, bright people will suffer him and look for the quickest opportunity to leave.

If you have a say in forming your team, make sure that you have people with different mindsets and different skill sets on the team so that strengths complement weaknesses and the team as a whole becomes strong. The tendency to choose people who are like you can spell disaster for a team. If everyone is like you, their weaknesses will be compounded. There will be too many people for one type of work and too few or none for another.

I used to always wonder about how much authority should I show as the leader of a team. After much thought and discussions with many people, we came up with this formula that I call the Authority Equation.

If a project is not too critical, and you have a very experienced team, show little to no authority. When people can manage work without your inputs, let them. This will empower them tremendously and infuse in them the fact that you trust them.

On the other hand, if the project is critical and the team is green, you will need to exercise a lot of authority, spelling out to people what they need to do and providing support to make sure they deliver.

When you bring a person on board your team, the first thing to do is to clarify what their compensation for working with you will be. Make sure that what you offer them feels fair to them and to you. If it doesn't, they will not perform optimally, or you will expect too much from them. Get that out of the way right at the beginning.

Second, bring about a sense of purpose in them. They need to know the big picture and where they fit in, and that the work they are doing really matters.

Here is a story that lays it out quite well. Two masons were cutting stones. One looked depressed, tired and utterly uninterested in the work that he was doing. The other had a radiant smile on his face and was totally focused on his work. Both were asked what they were doing.

The first one said, 'I am cutting stones.'

The second one said, 'I am building a cathedral!'

Create opportunities for people to grow in their work. In their time working with you, they should gain mastery in their role. Tremendous satisfaction comes from a job well done.

Once someone has become really good at what they do, get out of the way. Give them autonomy. This is the only effective way I know of to manage people who are far better than you in what they do.

Create a sense of safety for the people working with you. Take full responsibility if the team fails and pass on the credit to them if they succeed. If they don't feel safe informing you about a problem that may be brewing, it may well become an unmanageable catastrophe by the time you come to know about it.

I run the café at our ashram. We started with just three people, all of them hotel management graduates. First, I invited them to a meal cooked by me. Once that wowed them, I asked them if they would like to learn the way I cook. It was completely different from their formal training. I explained that I didn't want our café to serve 'hotel' food, I wanted it to taste like a really well-cooked 'home' meal.

Once they understood the vision for the café, they learnt very quickly. Over time, we got around thirty more people to join us. These were simple village folk. All of them had almost no background in cooking but they were willing to learn. They were slowly but surely trained. We started a fledging bakery to make simple cakes. We took on birthday and wedding catering jobs and our repertoire kept growing.

Once at a birthday party, while making butter paneer, the chef left the paneer in the tandoor a little bit longer than he should have. The paneer was charred a bit, and there was just no time to make anything else. My team was in a bit of a panic when they reported this to me. There was very little that could be done to salvage the butter paneer. In a flash of inspiration I just changed the label to 'Smoked Butter Paneer'! Everyone loved the earthy, smoky taste the slightly charred paneer infused in the sauce and the dish was a hit.

Turning a problem into an opportunity is a leader's job. Many times, leadership is simply the ability to disguise panic. Quick thinking can salvage most situations or turn them to your advantage. My practice of meditation really comes in handy at these times. It keeps me calm and collected in the midst of a tough situation and allows me to take effective action.

From serving a few simple snacks, we have now grown to serving full meals that include cuisines from around the world. We have even built our own wood-fired oven, and our fresh pizzas and breads are the talk of the town.

After a few years everything had begun to run smoothly enough to go by itself, and now we show profits even when I am travelling for months on end. I just monitor the team from time to time and show them interesting new recipes I come across. Giving people the space to make mistakes and learn from them is an integral part of being a leader.

These days, I am proud to report that they have started teaching me stuff!

You may wonder where I learnt all this. Amazingly, quite a few of these lessons were things I learnt by participating in extra-curricular activities during my time at IIT Bombay. Once I managed to win the inter-hostel freshman dramatics and music competitions, the seniors who were in charge of our hostel's cultural activities willingly gave me opportunities to play bigger roles in the inter-institute competitions.

①

PARTY LIST

Hemanshu Parekh
Neel Shah
Kedar Sohoni

- Clean the house
- Menu : Tomato Soup
  Tzatziki with Carrot slivers
  White Sauce baked veggies
  Dhansakh
  Chocolate Cake
  Ice cream with hot chocolate Sauce
  (Vanilla)

- Finger food : Gone in a gulp
  Paneer Tikka with green chutney
  Mango Margharita
  (Keep glasses ready, salted rims)

- Music – Light Classical & Pop
  Few hindi old Songs.

- Old photos from school & college

- Movies – Star Wars, Back to the Future,
  Avatar

- Gifts : Sai Symphonic cd, Gurudev's Knowledge sheets

Original Party List

②

PARTY LIST

Hemanshu Parekh (Read up on them, know names
Neel Shah   of wives & children (Jay)
Kedar Sohoni (Get some dji & pans for Sohoni)
- Decorate the house - flowers in Vases, rangoli outside, few
- Clean the house (Vacuum the sofas & curtains) candle
                    dust all the shelves
- Menu : Tomato Soup
  Bread   Tzatziki with Carrot slivers (Make sure there is
  & garlic butter   White Sauce baked veggies Dhansakh months
                     Dhansakh Tomato & Cucumber salad from
                     Chocolate Cake + lime slices Bombay)
  nuts to sprinkle Ice cream with hot chocolate Sauce
              (Vanilla) - Dinner on Terrace- set the terrace
- Finger food : Gone in a gulp   chairs, candles, plates, cutlery
  (get enough   Paneer Tikka with green chutney
   toothpicks) Mango Margharita
  Bruschetta with (Keep glasses ready, salted rims)
  tomato basil on crushed
              springs
- Music – Light Classical & Pop some meditation
  make playlist & Few hindi old Songs. with Gurudev?
  put on ipad
- Old photos from school & college
- Piano - practice a few pieces, ready to play for everyone
- Movies – Star Wars, Back to the Future, (Smilin
  decorations, Avatar, Andre Rieu, Andrea Bocelli Prayer, Taj
- Gifts : Sai Symphonic cd, Gurudev's Knowledge sheets
                                    (Chopin both)
- Board Game - Mumbai Connection

Modified Party List

③

TOMORROW'S TO DO.

- Sadhana: Padmasadhana, Kriya, Sahaj

- Exercise : 10 Surya namaskars
             Walk to Gurudev

- Write Blog post for Navrastri

- Write and finish mind mapping chapter
  for Book

- Gowri's house for lunch

- Email & facebook

- Get PS3 fixed

- Finish scheduling of Courses till Jan.

- Book air tickets to Delhi in March

- Drawings for CST - finish as many
                     as possible

- Read up CST notes.

- 11 am CST treatment

Original To-Do List

④

TOMORROW'S TO DO.

- Sadhana   Padmasadhana, Kriya, Sahaj
             Chant Gayatri & Om Namah Shivaya
- Exercise : 10 Surya namaskars with mantras
            (13)
            Walk to Gurudev
- Read me chapter of Bhagavad Geeta
- Write Blog post for Navrastri

- Write and finish mind mapping chapter
  for Book, get Niyati and Gauri's lists
- Gowri's house for lunch - Remember to
                            take Dinner set
- Email & facebook

- Get PS3 fixed
- More detailing for Bird Tv show with Abhi & Gauri
- Finish scheduling of Courses till Jan.

- Book air tickets to Delhi in March

- Drawings for CST - finish as many
                     as possible
- Meeting with Cafe guys for Navrastri teachers.
- Read up CST notes.
- Windows to be putted brown
- 11 am CST treatment
- Talk to carpenter to finish work in next 3 days

Modified To-Do List

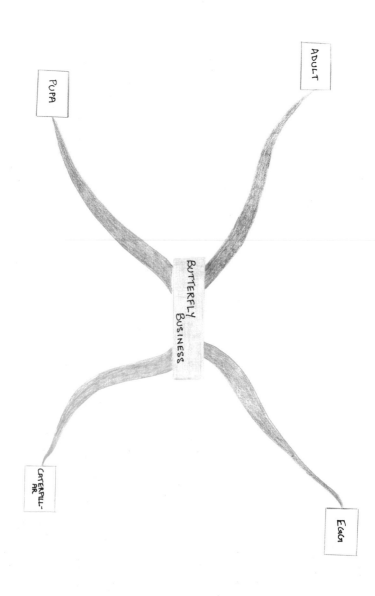

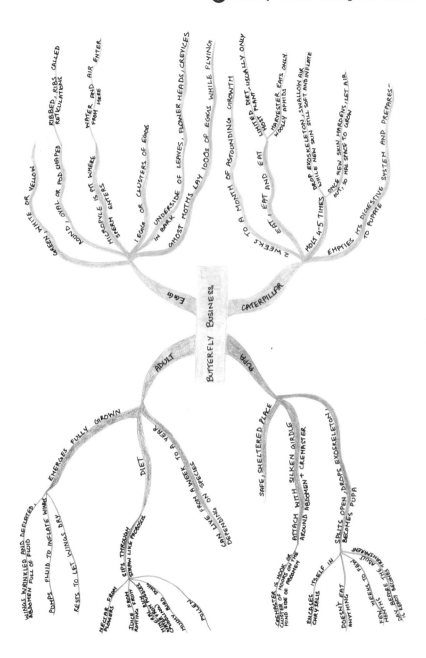

BUTTERFLY BUSINESS

EGG

- GREEN, WHITE OR YELLOW
- ROUND, OVAL OR POD SHAPED
- RIBBED, RIBS CALLED RETICULATIONS
- MICROPYLE IS PIT WHERE SPERM ENTERS
  - WATER AND AIR ENTER FROM HERE
- 1 EGG OR CLUSTERS OF EGGS
- UNDERSIDE OF LEAVES, FLOWER HEADS, CREVICES IN BARK
- GHOST MOTHS LAY 1000s OF EGGS WHILE FLYING

CATERPILLAR

- 2 WEEKS TO A MONTH OF ASTOUNDING GROWTH
- EATS, EATS AND EAT
  - LIMITED DIET, USUALLY ONLY 1 HOST PLANT
  - HARVESTER EATS WOOLLY APHIDS ONLY
- MOLTS 4-5 TIMES
  - DROP EXOSKELETON, SWALLOW AIR, WHILE NEW SKIN STILL SOFT AND INFLATE
  - ONCE NEW SKIN HARDENS, LET AIR OUT, SO HAS SPACE TO GROW
- EMPTIES ITS DIGESTIVE SYSTEM AND PREPARES TO PUPATE

ADULT

- EMERGES FULLY GROWN
  - WINGS WRINKLED AND DEFLATED, ABDOMEN FULL OF FLUID
  - PUMPS FLUID TO INFLATE WINGS
  - RESTS TO LET WINGS DRY
- DIET
  - NECTAR FROM FLOWERS
  - JUICE FROM ROTTING FRUIT
  - SIPS THROUGH STRAW LIKE PROBOSCIS
  - [illegible]
  - POLLEN
- LIVE FROM A WEEK TO A YEAR DEPENDING ON SPECIES

PUPA

- SAFE, SHELTERED PLACE
- ATTACH WITH SILKEN GIRDLE AROUND ABDOMEN + CREMASTER
  - CREMASTER IS HOOK OR CLUSTER OF HOOKS ON THE HIND END OF ABDOMEN
- SPLITS OPEN, DROPS EXOSKELETON, BECOMES PUPA
  - ENCASES ITSELF IN CHRYSALIS
  - DOESN'T EAT ANYTHING
  - FEW WEEKS TO A MONTH OR ABOUT A YEAR
  - [illegible] BEFORE THEY DRY, REDDY BLOODED TRANSPARENT

TASTES WITH THEIR FEET, NO MOUTHS

NEED SUN TO FLY, CAN'T FLY IN COLD

CAN SEE COLOURS RED, YELLOW, GREEN

LIGHT REFRACTS OFF THE SCALES SO WE CAN SEE THE COLOURS

WINGS ARE TRANSPARENT WITH TINY SCALES

THEIR SKELETONS ARE OUTSIDE THEIR BODY

WINGS WRINKLED AND DEFLATED. ABDOMEN FULL OF FLUID

PUMPS FLUID TO INFLATE WINGS

RESTS TO LET WINGS DRY.

EMERGES FULLY GROWN

NECTAR FROM FLOWERS

SIPS THROUGH STRAW LIKE PROBOSCIS

DIET

ADULT

BUTTERFLY

COOL

JUICE FROM ROTTING FRUIT

MINERAL RICH WATER FROM PUDDLES/ PUDDLING MUSHY BIRD DUNG

POLLEN

CAN LIVE FROM A WEEK TO A YEAR DEPENDING ON SPECIES

CREMASTER

SAFE, SHELTERED PLACE

PUPA

CREMASTER IS HOOK OR CLUSTER OF HOOKS ON THE HIND SIDE OF ABDOMEN

ATTACH WITH SILKEN GIRDLE AROUND ABDOMEN + CREMASTER

ENCASES ITSELF IN CHRYSALIS

DOESN'T EAT ANYTHING

SPLITS OPEN, DROPS EXOSKELETON BECOMES PUPA

FEW WEEKS TO FEW MONTHS

DAY BEFORE THE ADULT IS READY BECOMES TRANSPARENT

MATING

VISUAL CLUES AND PHEROMONES

ON GROUND OR IN AIR

MALE TRANSFERS SPERMATOPHORE IN FEMALE

INTERNAL FERTILIZATION FROM FEW SECONDS TO FEW HOURS

few sec to few hrs

BUSINESS

EGG

GREEN, WHITE OR YELLOW

ROUND, OVAL OR POD SHAPED

RIBBED; RIBS CALLED RETICULATIONS

WATER AND AIR ENTER FROM HERE

MICROPYLE IS PIT WHERE SPERM ENTERS

1 EGG OR CLUSTERS OF EGGS

UNDERSIDE OF LEAVES, FLOWER HEADS, CREVICES IN BARK

GHOST MOTH LAYS 1000s OF EGGS WHILE FLYING

CATERPILLAR

SILK PAD

CREMASTER

ABDOMINAL SEGMENTS

2 WEEKS TO A MONTH OF ASTOUNDING GROWTH

EAT, EAT AND EAT

2W

2m

LIMITED DIET, USUALLY ONLY HOST PLANT

HARVESTER EATS ONLY WOOLLY APHIDS

MOLT 4-5 TIMES

DROP EXOSKELETON; SWALLOW AIR WHILE NEW SKIN STILL SOFT AND INFLATE

ONCE NEW SKIN HARDENS, LET AIR OUT, SO HAS SPACE TO GROW

EMPTIES ITS DIGESTIVE SYSTEM AND PREPARES TO PUPATE

1000s

STRAIN AND RESERVE WATER

LEMON SIZED BALL OF TAMARIND;

SOAK FOR 30 MINUTES

PUREE 9 OF THEM

·30min·

12 MEDIUM SIZED TOMATOES;
WASHED AND PEELED

ROUGHLY CHOP 3 OF THEM

GOWRI'S UTTERLY [

10 CLOVES OF GARLIC; SLIGHTLY CRUSHED

DISSOLVE 1 HEAPED TBSP OF RASAM POWDER IN WATER

SERVE

3 RED CHILLIES

2 TSPS OF JEERA

1 TSP OF RAI

10 CURRY LEAVES

1/2 TSP

GARLIC / SAUTE TILL GOLDEN BROWN

...EE ; ADD

RASAM POWDER WATER

1/2 TSP TURMERIC POWDER + 3 PINCHES OF HING

HING

PUREED TOMATOES + 1L OF WATER

1 Ltr

CHOPPED TOMATOES , JAGGERY AND SALT TO TASTE

...US RASAM

...H WITH CHOPPED CORIANDER LEAVES

...NG HOT WITH FRESHLY COOKED RICE

W/

ADD A DOLLOP OF GHEE

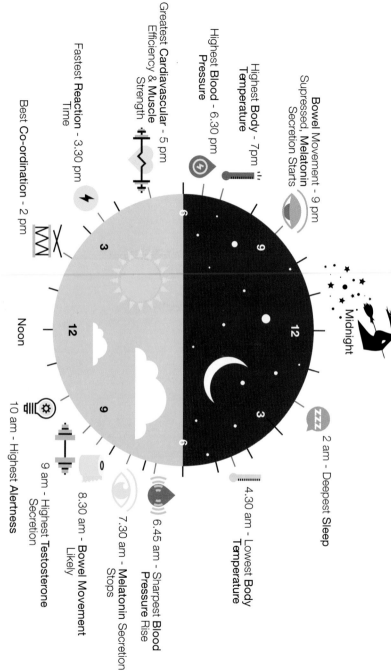

Bowel Movement Supressed, **Melatonin** Secretion Starts - 9 pm

Highest Body **Temperature** - 7pm

Highest Blood **Pressure** - 6.30 pm

Greatest **Cardiavascular** Efficiency & Muscle Strength - 5 pm

Fastest **Reaction** Time - 3.30 pm

Best **Co-ordination** - 2 pm

Noon

Midnight

2 am - Deepest Sleep

4.30 am - Lowest Body **Temperature**

6.45 am - Sharpest **Blood Pressure** Rise

7.30 am - **Melatonin** Secretion Stops

8.30 am - **Bowel Movement** Likely

9 am - Highest **Testosterone** Secretion

10 am - Highest **Alertness**

Most of what I have written above was acquired from being part of teams that performed, won and lost in the intra- and inter-institute competitions.

It was all great fun and superb learning.

Later, as a full-time Art of Living volunteer and teacher, I have worked in quite a few teams and been in charge of many more. Dinesh and I have handled teams for many different types of projects.

We have been involved in:

Creating Art of Living's YES!+ workshop and coaching over 1,000 trainers to teach it. It has been taught in more than 100 countries and lakhs of young people have benefitted from it.

Running Café Vishala.

Organizing huge events (in excess of 20,00,000 people) for Gurudev.

Anti-tobacco drives.

Planting more than 10,000 trees in less than a year.

Cleaning up slums.

Interventions in high-security prisons.

Organizing fundraising events for children's education.

Creating a suicide helpline that has saved many lives.

Making short films and videos.

Creating a music CD called Sri Symphonic Bhajans.

Making a board game called Mumbai Connection, to mention a few.

Just organizing and teaching Art of Living courses gave me invaluable insights into leadership and team management. We have personally been instrumental in bringing the knowledge and techniques of the Art of Living to excess of 5,00,000 people.

This meant dealing with many different types of people.

You can imagine the number of things that have gone wrong or could have gone awry while making all this happen. I could write an entire book on it.

Fair compensation, instilling a sense of purpose, giving opportunities for mastery, granting autonomy and generating a feeling of safety are the cornerstones of my secrets of creating and leading great teams!

Stories with Gurudev

However, some of the best lessons about team management I have learnt, and am still learning, are from Gurudev himself.

Some time ago, Dinesh and I had been posted outside India to organize a huge event for Gurudev. There was one lady, an experienced volunteer, who seemed to be almost sabotaging the event. She tried our patience in every way possible, creating obstacles where there should have been none. When I talked to Gurudev about her and said she had become a real pain and that short of confronting her and telling her that her attitude was detrimental to the event and the organization, I had no idea how to deal with her, he said something very interesting.

Instead of confronting her, as I had planned to, he told me to tell her that I didn't like the way others talked about her because of her behaviour. That she was so experienced and senior and the gossip that was making the rounds about her hurt me.

When I did that, there was an almost magical transformation in her!

When a behavioural change is called for, tell the people concerned about what's in it for them. How they will benefit by their change of attitude. For most people this method works really well.

Another time, I was sitting with Gurudev in his meeting room when a few very angry people walked in. I got up to leave and he motioned me to stay. I sat in a corner and observed an entire drama unfold before me.

The first lot of angry people were parents of children studying in one of our fledging schools. They complained that the teachers were not good enough, that the principal never had time to meet them and hear their grievances and that they had trusted the Art of Living name and so enrolled their children in our school. They were feeling extremely let down. For more than forty minutes, Gurudev simply listened to them and let them vent. He gently told them that he would look into the issue.

From my corner, I felt that the lives of these young children shouldn't be played around with … that we should definitely get better teachers and another principal. I totally empathized with the parents.

Next came the group of teachers of that school. They had another round of complaining. How they were overworked, their salaries didn't come on time, how belligerent the principal was and how ungrateful the parents were and how all their efforts were never recognized or appreciated by anyone. As I heard the teachers over the next forty minutes, I started feeling that the parents had no gratitude for the hard work that these sincere people were doing. The principal didn't seem to be doing her job. I felt a lot of sympathy for these teachers. Gurudev neither agreed nor disagreed. He remained totally neutral and simply listened.

Last came the principal. She talked softly and said the parents expected to meet her at their convenience; they would walk into the school and demand her time. Many wouldn't turn up for the PTA meets. She admitted that the teachers' salaries had been delayed and that she would make sure that issue would be sorted. She said that there were teething problems and that she would make sure things got better. Now, I felt that here is a lady who is so reasonable and mature. She takes responsibility and has confidence. I felt the parents and teachers were at fault for blaming this wonderful person. Gurudev listened to her assurances and still maintained his air of utter neutrality.

When she left, Gurudev called me to his side and asked me what I had learnt from the past two hours. I told him how my opinions completely changed as I heard each group. I found myself in total agreement with each party as they spoke their side of the story.

He said that as a leader it's our responsibility to give a neutral hearing to all sides of any story before taking any decision. There is not much point in hearing out the others if you have already decided who is at fault. It's supremely important to maintain neutrality and not give in to the tendency to side with the person who got to you first.

Listening with neutrality to all sides of any story before taking any decision or siding with any one party has helped me make, many fair and just decisions.

A few times, some team I was leading simply didn't listen to what I asked them to do. The exact same instruction from Gurudev would make them jump into action. Sometimes Gurudev even used the very same words I had used. When I would say it, not much would move. When he said it, magic happened.

I asked him once how this was possible.

With a twinkle in his eyes, he said, 'It's not about what's being said, it's all about who is saying it.'

I will leave you to think about that. I am thinking about it too.

Evolving into a beloved leader is an art that may need to be practiced for lifetimes. Meanwhile, go participate in that play or that soccer match. Sometimes, work can wait!

ROCKING RELATIONSHIPS

Why are we talking about relationships in a book about studying?

Healthy relationships make your endocrine system secrete all the right chemicals inside you, making you feel safe and secure. Your neurons love this feeling and in turn make you super productive, creative and efficient. Friends and loved ones are very precious. Relationships require nurturing and great relationships can be conducive when it comes to the generation of amazing work!

On the other hand, it can become incredibly difficult to focus on your work if some relationship has gone sour. Have a tiff with your best friend, one of your parents or anyone you really care for, and it becomes very tough to think geometry, organic chemistry, figures of speech or history.

Love can make things very complicated. There is a lot that can be wonderful when you are in love, but even in a very charitable mood, we cannot claim that falling in love is good for studying. You see that special person across the room, and there is a sudden strange sensation in your chest, your mind becomes coherently incoherent, your legs feel weak, there is something hot and cold all over your body. There is a lot that has been written about this phenomenon by people far more expressive than me, so I won't bother elaborating.

The best thing, of course, is to avoid the romance stuff totally while you are studying and save it up for later in life. Unfortunately, love doesn't believe in asking your permission. You are walking along, minding your business, when – bam! – love happens. Love can make wisdom and common sense vanish and break all the rules you have made for yourself. In those moments, algebra, geography, statistics and your upcoming exam will not seem to matter much anymore.

If you are one of the bammed, then definitely read on. For those of you who have not yet had a bam, read on anyway, I am sure you will find something relevant for you.

Giving and Taking

When my sister got married, my dad gave her a little box, which had 'Marriage' elaborately written on it. He told her if she put more into it than she would take out of it, the marriage would always be full. They have been through some very tough patches, but their relationship works because they follow this simple rule. Put more into the relationship than you take out.

In any relationship, there needs to be give and take. If you are only giving and not taking, you will make the other person feel obliged, and a person who feels obligated to you will not want to be around you. If you are only taking, then you become a parasite and no one will want to be with a parasite for too long. Giving and taking are integral in a relationship.

When you give, give generously. There is not much point in giving something you will not miss. That's not giving, that's just emptying your wardrobe.

Ever since he first did an Art of Living course with me, Jayesh had been volunteering his time and effort in organizing courses. He would always be there, managing the logistics that ensured the smooth delivery of workshops, consistently and silently working on the sidelines. He was, for a very long time, our man Friday. When he finally graduated after eight long years of slogging it out, I wanted to give him something really special. The only thing I had at that time was a brand-new laptop that Dinesh and I had saved up for, for almost a year. We both decided to give the laptop to Jayesh. We had one laptop between us for a long time and were enjoying having two, but Jayesh definitely deserved something nice. When we presented him his new toy, he was totally thrilled. It was the perfect graduation gift! When it's time to give, give with a magnanimous heart.

After an Art of Living course, my students would be so joyful and grateful that they would often bring gifts for me. I would refuse to accept any gift, telling them to donate for our children studying at the rural ashram schools instead. I did this for quite some time and once very proudly spoke about it to Gurudev. He gently rebuked me, saying that if I didn't accept the gifts they brought for me with such love, I would be breaking their hearts. It was only then that I realized how important it is to take. Learning to take graciously is a fundamental aspect of any relationship, and when I took the little gifts my students would bring me with grace, I found their connection with me become so much deeper and stronger.

The silver jubilee celebration of the Art of Living was a humungous event with over two million people participating. Many, many people contributed to the event with their time, money, skill and effort. An incident from that time is etched in my mind. It's about giving and taking.

One of the workers who was building the stage met Gurudev and handed over to him an envelope containing some money. He said he felt privileged that he was given the opportunity to be part of something so magnificent and apologized for not being able to contribute more. Gurudev looked into the envelope and quickly realized that this man was giving more than what he would earn in a month. Gurudev removed a ₹500 note from the envelope and returned the rest to the worker, saying these 500 rupees was very precious to Him. This was a fabulous reminder to me about giving generously and taking graciously.

Communicating

Sometimes, people simply don't talk to each other about things that matter. They assume a sort of sixth sense in the other person and get devastated when the other person fails to guess what was going on in their minds.

There was this young couple in a course I was once teaching; let's call them Rohit and Shilpa. They had been married for just a few months, and both were very pleasant and extremely smart. During the classes, they would sit in two different parts of the hall and at every opportunity would pass comments about each other. Most times these were harmless and everyone would have a great laugh, but sometimes from their faces I could make out that one of them had crossed some line and had hurt the other.

I asked them both to come up to the front and then asked both of them that if they could change one small thing in each other, what would it be? One had to listen while the other talked. There could be no interruptions.

Rohit insisted on going first. He looked at Shilpa and said, 'Every morning, when you serve me my toast at breakfast, you have this extremely irritating habit.' She looked at him quizzically as he went on, 'You remove the top and bottom slices of the bread, toast them, butter them and eat them yourself! Every morning I wait and think, "Maybe today she will give that crusty slice to me", and every morning I have to watch in disappointment as you gobble both of them up.' He then made puppy eyes while saying, 'Give me at least one of those slices...'

While Rohit was talking, Shilpa was beside herself, wanting to interrupt, but I held her back. She had to wait for her turn.

As soon as Rohit had finished talking, she blurted out, 'I HATE those crusty pieces. I love the soft bread. I didn't want you to eat that part of the bread because I love you, so every morning I would force myself to eat them because I didn't want to waste them...'

The entire class burst out clapping and laughing. They had been doing this for months! They are now having much better mornings, now that Rohit gets the crust and Shilpa gets her soft bread.

Do yourself and your friends a favour. Tell them what you are thinking, instead of expecting them to read your mind. Things will be much smoother.

Nastiness Should Wait, Niceness Shouldn't

When you want to say something nasty to someone, wait. Don't do it. Write out that email if you want, but don't press the send button. Don't make that phone call. Hold on.

In a little while, you are going to feel very different about the whole situation and if you have sent out the email, there is very little you will be able to do about it. Before communicating anything unpleasant to anyone, just wait for a few hours. Many relationships have been saved when people follow this simple rule.

Don't hold that nastiness in. Holding it in will make you feel terrible. Always make it a point to express the unpleasantness. Let it find expression in an email or a letter that you don't send. you will feel much better and a probable crack in a relationship will not happen.

Of course, if after some time you still feel the need to let the other person know, you are welcome to send that email you wrote. Please read it before you send it. Many times I have written a stinker and following my own rule didn't press the send button. When I get back to that email in a bit, I am always taken aback by how vitriolic I had been and a very few times, even when I felt I needed to send the email, I would tone it down a lot before sending it off.

When you want to say something nice to anyone, do it right away. Don't postpone thinking they know anyway and there is no point in telling them. Most times, a simple heartfelt thank you or I love you can deeply enhance a relationship.

A friend of ours, Shyam, had quite a rocky relationship with his father. There was a lot of love there, but there were also a lot of misunderstandings, bad communication and mistrust. This meant that they would avoid each other as much as they could. Their interactions would be brusque. Shyam would often come away feeling that a hug would fix things, but he never did it.

He did a course for enhancing relationships in which his homework was to tell his dad he loved him. It was to be done over the weekend. He went to his father's house on Saturday night but saw the old man peacefully sitting in his easy chair watching some TV, so decided not to disturb him and instead tell him on Sunday. There was no doubt in his head that he would tell his dad … but he thought, not tonight. Tomorrow.

His father died peacefully that night, and Shyam never got a chance to say that 'I love you' to him. He had tears in his eyes when he told us at the funeral, 'The bastard died on me!' Any time I have felt that I want to tell someone anything nice, I remember those words and do it right away. Life is very fragile. Be nice as often and as soon as you possibly can.

Ingenuity Is the Key

Ankita had been going around with Gaurav for quite some time before they found the time to get married. They made a brilliant couple. They were both attractive, smart and had a terrific sense of humour. It was a dream relationship. They were also very honest with each other and this caused a small problem. Gaurav made no secret about the fact that he liked to 'look at' other women. Frequently, while the two of them were together, his head would swivel around and he would let out a low appreciative whistle when he saw someone really good-looking pass by. For a long time, Ankita didn't mind this much.

She knew in his heart Gaurav only wanted her. She was also very grateful that he didn't hide this from her and do it behind her back. But over time, she started having self-doubts. When she talked about this to Gaurav, he couldn't understand why this 'harmless' habit of his had suddenly become such a big issue...

Ankita came to me and told me all about it. He was not going to change, this was clear. She was getting more and more distressed, this was also clear. I gave her a super simple solution. Every time he did it, she should follow his gaze and start to admire the outfit or the jewellery the other woman was wearing. Then, she was to start pleading with him for a dress or jewellery just like it. That other woman was looking so nice in it. She would too.

She got him to spend quite a lot of money this way until he realized that his 'harmless' pass time was becoming quite expensive. Ankita really enjoyed herself for a few weeks. Gaurav doesn't look at any woman, however beautiful, any more. He cannot afford it.

Sometimes what can seem to be a huge problem can be easily resolved, with a little bit of skill, patience, ingenious thinking and humour.

Time and Space

Yeah, it's still about relationships. Don't worry, I am not going quantum on you. The most precious commodity that all of us have is time. Anything and everything else has the possibility of coming back. Not time. Time spent is lost forever. The biggest way you can show someone you care is to spend time with them. Spending time with them doesn't mean sitting next to them and texting on a mobile or watching a movie they are not interested in. Really being with them matters. It need not even be about talking. Sometimes it's enough just to be close.

A few people can go overboard with this, however. They want to spend so much time with people they care about that those people want to get away from them. While spending that precious commodity with the people you love, also remember to give them space so they can choose to do stuff they want to do without you hovering around. Without space, things can become quite claustrophobic and destroy beautiful relationships.

There is no formula about how much time should be spent and how much space needs to be given. Every person is unique and each relationship is different. It is a fine balance and you need to figure it out for every person you care for.

Fights and Flights

Prama and Ranji Bhandari have been married fifty-five years. When asked the secret of their wonderful marriage, they both agree that it is because they fight. They find new things to fight about and fight for. It keeps them young. It keeps them fit. It keeps them on their toes. When you see the two of them together, you know they are still very much in love, even after fifty-five years. Their real secret is that they never interpret an argument to mean that the other person doesn't love them or care for them.

I may not like what you are saying or doing, but this shouldn't get equated with: you don't love me, respect me or care for me. If you can train your mind to not jump to the conclusion that the other person doesn't care simply because they are doing or saying something you don't like, your relationship will be safe.

Dinesh comes from a very conservative Maharashtrian family. When he decided to become a teacher for the Art of Living at the age of nineteen, his parents were in shock. His mother, especially, simply couldn't accept that her son would not be doing all the 'regular' things that sons should be doing in their lives.

There were tantrums, emotional blackmail and shouting matches galore that Dinesh bore with patience and his quiet simplicity. In time, his parents gave in to Dinesh's wishes but were still not happy about it. They totally blamed me for waylaying their son. Curiosity got them onto an Art of Living course with me. After learning to meditate and practising for some time, his mother came to another course that I was teaching and towards the end of the course asked permission to speak. I was quite apprehensive about what she was going to say but nevertheless handed the mike over to her.

She told everyone about the drama at home. She said Maharashtrians believed that Gyaneshwar (a saint) should definitely be born, but not in their own house. Saints should take birth in the neighbour's home. Everyone laughed. She spoke for some time about all the mental gymnastics her mind did when she realized her son was going to be an Art of Living teacher and would not be going off to the US to get a job and eventually get married. She concluded by saying that before she learnt to meditate, her family – husband and three children – were her world. Now the whole world was her family!

If you throw a small stone into a bucket of water, there is so much turbulence that's created. Throw a huge boulder in a lake and it will make a few waves and then settle to the bottom. In a while, the boulder will not even be noticed; while in the bucket, the stone will stick out like a sore thumb.

Families and smaller groups of friends can have so many issues with each other. It's because the focus is too narrow. A small challenge seems to be insurmountable and cause of so much grief and stress, just like the stone in the bucket. Expand your sphere and feel the whole world is your family. Then even a boulder-like situation will fail to bother you.

Having goals bigger than yourselves can make relationships last forever. When the focus is on each other, nit-picking happens and a dream becomes a nightmare. When the focus is on something much bigger, then you wake up and realize the wonder of each other, and a relationship truly blossoms.

A few times things can go terribly wrong. Heartache can be a horrible experience. Here, the only thing that works is to take up a hobby to occupy yourself while you give yourself the time to recover from a broken, vandalized heart. Do something creative. Keep your mind busy.

Meditation, yoga and pranayama will help big time and hasten the process of making the pain go away. Woody Allen once said that comedy is just tragedy plus time. Give yourself time and pretty soon you will be able to laugh with all your being all over again…

A young fellow once asked Gurudev – How do I concentrate on my studies and my work when all the beautiful girls around me are constantly diverting my attention? All I want to do is look at them. Not my books. What should I do?

Gurudev laughed and replied, 'Make sure you look at those books, otherwise none of the beautiful girls will look at you!'

SUICIDE IS NOT AN OPTION

It was past midnight on a cold winter night. Everything that could have possibly gone wrong had managed to go wrong and in the most dramatic way. I had yet again flunked. My stock in IIT had dipped substantially. In a place where grades are God, getting an F was sure to make you a social pariah, even if you happened to be a very nice person who was superbly talented in things other than academics.

My best friend had found a girlfriend and didn't have any time for me any more. I was far away from my piano and my music. I had not yet learnt to meditate. The future looked very bleak. I was miserable, lonely and fed up with life.

There was some demon in my mind that was feeding my thoughts with all the negativity that it could.

Almost automatically, without thinking, I found myself walking out of our hostel and along the road that led to the lake. Someone called out to me but I ignored him. The trees cast long ominous shadows as wind whistled through them and there was a ghostly mist. I walked alone in the chill night air, shivering slightly.

I reached the lake. City lights twinkled in the distance. There were millions of people with millions of dreams and hopes out there. But I was alone. There didn't seem any hope for me. There was some sort of roaring sound in my ears. The dark waters of the lake lapped the shore silently, inviting me in.

I took a hesitant step towards the water. Something was holding me back, but I shook it off. Enough of this life. Another more determined step. And another…

I resolutely went into the water and had a shock. The water was too cold. Somehow it woke me up. Brought me back to my senses. The roaring in my mind stopped and was replaced by calm serene feeling.

Life is for living.

And then my customary sense of humour took over. I told myself there was no way I was going to drown in this ridiculously cold water. Too uncomfortable. Me, who would make such a fuss about taking a bath in anything other than piping hot water, committing suicide in the middle of winter in cold water?! Unthinkable!

I grinned and then laughed. Suddenly, all the good wonderful things I had been blessed with flashed through my mind. Warmth enveloped me as I made my way back to the hostel.

The mist seemed inviting and friendly; the trees seemed to be sighing in relief.

I went back to my hostel, to my friends, to my books and to my life. Somehow, things didn't seem to be so terrible any more.

I was lucky. Many aren't.

Suicide is simply not an option. It is always completely out of the question. Suicide is a spiritual crime and is the absolutely worst thing you can do to yourself.

However bad life gets, suicide will only make it worse. When you drop the body, you don't drop the mind. That comes along with you. When you have the body and you are feeling terrible, stressed, angry, tired, depressed, there is so much you can do. You can scream, shout, cry, lash out … You can express your grief in so many ways.

Just imagine the exact same state of mind, all the misery, turmoil, frustration, sadness … but at the same time, without a body to be able to express them. Suicide does that. It takes away the body, but it leaves you with an overwhelmingly disturbed mind and no way to free yourself from that distress. No way to sob or shout or express anything. Just a ball of black negativity.

Your worst nightmare is nothing compared to what happens to you if you commit suicide.

Suicide is karmic catastrophe.

Our scriptures say that when we die, our soul stays in limbo for a maximum of thirteen days. This is not a pleasant place to be in. Most souls stay there for a very brief period of time and then move on to other higher realms, other planes of existence. But a person who commits suicide can stay in this limbo realm for a few hundred years. If and when they finally manage to get a body again, it is usually deformed and they are condemned to live through circumstances far worse than they were in when they took their own lives.

People resort to suicide to get relief from pain. Paradoxically, they forget that relief is a feeling and they need to be alive to feel it.

Suicide is an extreme form of depression. The reasons for the depression could be anything, ranging from disappointment in love, business or academics, to anything else as well. The resulting pain and stress lead to feelings of emptiness and hopelessness, to illness due to chemical imbalances in the brain.

Bad grades or business decisions and failures are just mistakes. Learn from them and move on. Sooner or later you will succeed. And what if someone who you love doesn't love you back? Don't bother thinking about it; that simply means they have bad taste. Nature is saving you up for someone really special! Move on…

Depression basically stems from the question 'What about me?'

Feeling suicidal indicates very low energy levels and no wisdom. People think of suicide when pain seems to exceed the resources available for coping with that pain. People having such thoughts are not weak, crazy, flawed or lacking in will power. It may not even mean that they actually want to die. It simply means they have more pain than they can cope with right now. There are many kinds of pain that may lead to suicide. What may be bearable to someone may be unbearable to someone else.

Suicide is damaging the body to put an end to mental pain. That's like putting a Band-Aid on your toe hoping it will make your headache go away. Or removing all your clothes because you are feeling very cold.

There are two ways of dealing with suicidal thoughts. One is to increase your ability to bear pain, the other increase your resource base. Both are possible. One of the simplest ways I know to make both happen is learning and practising meditation and doing some sort of social service. Meditation will help you quickly snap out of it.

The most authentic thing about us human beings is our capacity to love, to laugh, to create, to overcome, to endure, to transform and to be greater than whatever challenges life throws at us.

Gurudev once said, 'Pain is inevitable, suffering is optional.'

There are always reasons to be thankful if you look hard enough for them. Even if there has been darkness for a thousand years in some place, it doesn't take a thousand years to bring light. One lit candle can dispel a thousand years of darkness in less than a second. Once even a spark of gratitude comes, in no time it becomes a blazing fire and all these thoughts vanish like dew on a hot summer morning.

When I wrote an article about suicide on my blog a few years ago, Ashwani commented on it. I reproduce that comment here almost verbatim:

Few months back I had this strong feeling to commit suicide again …What helped me out this time were three things:

1. The scenes from *Munnabhai M.B.B.S* and *Lage Raho Munnabhai*

One place Munna shouts at a young guy in a hospital who attempted suicide over failed love – 'For a girl you met ninety days back, you are going to kill yourself … Can't you live for your mother who has loved you for nineteen years?' (Sounds better in Hindi.)

In *Lage Raho Munnabhai*, he says to another young man who has lost ₹ 7 lakhs of his father's life savings in shares and is contemplating suicide – 'Don't talk nonsense! You think your father will be overjoyed when he sees your lifeless body? The same shoulders on which he carried you when you were a child will carry your dead body. How do you think it will make him feel? Proud? Arrey, for months he won't even believe that you have died … He will dial your phone number again and again hoping to hear your voice…'

2. I used to think that I am a very weak person because I was thinking of suicide and that made me feel even worse … until I read a part of *Autobiography of a Yogi*, even Swami Paramahamsa thought of 'hurling his body in front of a speeding train'. If he can have such feelings then me having the same feelings is utterly forgivable.
3. One of my friends Pradeep died in a bike accident some years ago. I'll never forget how inconsolable and shattered his parents were when they saw his battered body. I will never knowingly do that to my parents or to the people who I love or who love me. I am not THAT selfish!

I have one question though, Bau, I sometimes wonder why people meet with such terrible consequences. Even when they are spiritual and meditate, sometimes they die in such a tragic way. Why does this happen? I cannot understand this.

I replied to him:

We all die, whether it is through some disease or an accident, young or old, death is certain … We usually want to do all the negative things immediately. Getting angry, badmouthing someone, gossiping. We want to do that now.

Life is fragile and this is all the more reason not to postpone the important things in life … saying I love you, and thank you, smiling and laughing and singing and dancing and meditating and going for walks and flying kites and playing and studying (!) and doing as many advance courses (the Art of Living Advanced

Meditation Courses) as you possibly can, spending more time with the people who truly matter.

Postponing the bad stuff and doing all the good stuff right away is a fantastic habit.

Spirituality is not here to save you from death. Spirituality helps you enjoy life. For a spiritual person, (natural) death is simply a longer sleep than usual.

Spirituality makes sure that if and when you do come back, you have a say in it. When you are enlightened, you don't have to come back. You choose to come back and play with life.

Death is the ultimate adventure. But like all good things, you have to wait for it to happen; otherwise it becomes a tragedy and a calamity. Work, play, love, live, laugh, sing, dance, meditate, do some social service and most importantly, quieten your mind.

This will make you happy, peaceful, satisfied and successful in the Here and the Hereafter!

NO JOB? SO WHAT?

Possibly the luckiest thing that can happen to you is that you don't get a job!

I have watched my parents work nine-to-five jobs all their lives. Dad worked for almost twenty years with Godrej, and then another fifteen with the Tatas. Mom worked at a single job all through her life, at ICICI. My sister and I have had a very comfortable life because of their dedication to their jobs.

But quite early in life, I had decided that this sort of a life is definitely not for me. I had no idea what I would do, but I knew that I wouldn't do a job. After my master's at IIT, I didn't even sit for campus placements because I was so clear that I was not going to do a job. For me, Art of Living became my calling. I have been with Gurudev and Art of Living for more than twenty-five years now, though the reasons why I chose Art of Living (or maybe it was the other way round) are a story for another time.

I know working in a big organization can give a great sense of security and many times, tremendous satisfaction. To be part of something big and grand can be quite thrilling; but nonetheless, for the smartosapien, it would just be a waste of time. For the ones with stars in their eyes, a job should be a worst-case scenario. In case everything fails, and there is nothing left to do, then take up a job.

India is a land ripe with such amazing opportunities.

How about a profession in adventure sports? Or tourism? Farming? Maybe teaching yoga. Or creating that restaurant you have always dreamed about. Taking an online course or two and learning some new skill ... website programming or video editing. Interior design? Exploring alternative medicine? 3D animation? Making a board game, creating your own brand of clothes?

Your reality is only limited by your own imagination!

Let me tell you a few stories.

A friend of mine – let's call her Rekha – loved shopping. Her husband was a small-time builder, and they were doing quite well. Their marriage was fantastic and everything was great, except for Rekha's shopping bills, which her husband found extravagant, which led to many good-natured pokes and fights.

On a visit to London, Rekha was wearing a beautiful shawl that she had picked up in Nepal. A friend of hers fell in love with it and insisted that she sell it to her. Rekha, being the wife of a businessman, sold it at a very good profit.

This deal gave her an idea. When she returned to India, in the winter months she travelled all over the country picking up wonderful artisan-made knick-knacks and all sort of beautiful clothes. Her passion for shopping had made her a keen observer and a fabulous bargainer.

Next summer, Rekha went to London again and this time around, at a friend's house, she organized a sale of the stuff she had bought in India. Just a quiet little thing between friends and the friends of friends. It was a super hit! Her taste was impeccable and everyone loved her collection. Everything was sold out in two days and she made a huge profit!

And so, she started her little business. She would travel all around India, making friends with artisan dealers of exotic goods and buying from them. She would travel first class to London and sell most of that (keeping the absolute best for herself) to her hungry clientele in the UK. She had married her passion for shopping to a cool business idea and was getting paid for what she thoroughly enjoyed doing. She got to shop. Her husband didn't have to foot her bills any more. Her friends in London got a taste of the India that they so sorely missed. She gave very good prices to the artisans she was buying from. It was win-win-win all along.

Another friend, Kapil, was so inspired listening to me about doing business instead of doing a job that he decided to start a business of his own. Unfortunately, that utterly flopped, landing him in debt. He started another venture that became another failure, landing him with even more debt. He started many more, each one failing more spectacularly than the previous one.

He did some really crazy stuff. A few years ago, in a sort of desperation to pay off his debt, he bought 2-3 tons of onions at very cheap rates when the prices of onions had sky-rocketed, hoping to sell them off at a huge profit. Of course the plan failed and he stored all the onions in his house, which in a few days one could smell from a mile.

In our circle, it became a joke. We would laugh at him and tease him mercilessly, but he just wouldn't give up. He had the last laugh when he created a workshop for budding entrepreneurs about what NOT to do when you are starting a business. It was very funny, from the heart and full of absolutely the most important things you should watch out for when starting out on your own. It's wildly successful and has managed to pay off all his debts, and it has given him time to do what he really wanted to do in the first place – teach Art of Living courses!

Prasanth came to work with us at the ashram. He felt his engineering studies were a waste of time and dropped out after the second year. He wanted to spend time with Dinesh and me and do some 'internetseva' with us. He knew how to make websites. He stayed in the ashram for a few years with us, making all the YES!⁺ websites as well as developing our blog www.bawandinesh.in. On the side, he would take a few programming projects from various online websites and earn a 'bit' of money. Later we learnt that he used to earn more than Rs 50k a month working a few hours in the nights, few days a week, after he had finished his official work!

Due to some tragedies in his family, he was forced to relocate back to Kerala, where he opened up a small internet-based development start-up. He now employs more than ten people and singlehandedly manages to support two entire families who are dependent on him. Of late he has even been talking about shifting back to where he belongs – our ashram.

Dr Spandan is a dentist. Or rather, she was. She was a first class student and a brilliant dentist when she used to practice dentistry. While she was studying dentistry, she had an injury to her spine, which left her mostly bound to a wheelchair. She managed to complete her dentistry programme, surviving on painkillers and in severe pain. She was also depressed. She was slated for surgery within a year, where titanium implants would be introduced into her spine to correct it. She had made a few suicide attempts that fortunately went hilariously wrong.

Her mother sent her off to do an Art of Living course hoping it would help. It did. She felt a whole lot better and the gloom in her head had cleared out a lot. Dinesh was her teacher and when she told him about all the things she was going through and her impending surgery, he asked her to meet Gurudev before going for the surgery. She came to meet Gurudev, who met her very briefly and suggested that she take CST.

She had no idea what CST (craniosacral therapy) was. Coincidentally, Bente from Denmark, who is a fantastic craniosacral therapist, was arriving at the ashram the very next day. Spandan scheduled an appointment with Bente and took CST over a period of around six months. She became totally all right through the treatment and actually did surya namaskars in front of her surgeon on the day of her surgery. Needless to say, the surgery didn't happen and her spine is in brilliant shape.

Her interest in this alternative form of therapy was piqued and when Gurudev asked her to learn CST, she readily agreed, much to the dismay of her parents (her father is a retired army doctor and didn't believe in any sort of 'alternative' stuff), who wanted to see her established as a great dentist. Even her friends warned her against taking such a step, plunging into something that could be witchcraft, leaving a glittering career as a dentist in the wake.

She disregarded everyone and went ahead. She figured out that what she really wanted to do was heal people and reduce the pain in the world and saw a superb possibility in realizing that dream by becoming a CST practitioner.

There were no courses on CST on offer in India at the time, so she learnt from wherever she could and whoever would teach her. The ashram usually had someone from the West who knew the technique. She worked with those people and chewed their brains. Finally, she located an Australian institute who taught a certificate course in India and went for it. Two long years later, she was certified to practice. She continues to learn and hone her skills even now and over the last seven to eight years has treated thousands of people, relieving them of their pains and helping them overcome their traumas. She is living the life she always wanted to live.

Shilpi loves shoes and doodling. She would draw all sorts of cartoons all over the place. Her room was a study of crazy drawings that would change almost every time I would visit her house. And she was mad over shoes. I don't think even she knows how many pairs of shoes she has. Once, she doodled a design on her designer shoes and when her friends saw it, all of them wanted a doodle on their shoes too!

She suddenly became very busy. In about a year she had opened a tiny little shop for doing just this. Doodling and personalizing shoes.

She has trained a few people and now her business runs even when she is off travelling all over the world, which is her other passion.

I wonder how she is going to marry that with shoes and doodling!

Then there is   Chirag. Chirag Aggarwal, B.A. in English. When he actually managed to get that degree, whatever little faith I had in the Indian education system kind of evaporated.

He had trouble spelling trouble. His grammar was atrocious, but he was blissfully ignorant of that because of course he didn't know what atrocious was.

He was really astounded to find out that there was a 'z' in Czechoslovakia and utterly taken aback when he learnt that there was a 'p' in psychology. He didn't know the difference between a simile and a metaphor...

We had terrific fun at his expense! Abhi and Gowri have recorded videos of Chirag spelling stuff and you can hear hoots of laughter in the background as he would blunder about.

The wonderful part about him was that he would join us in the laughter. He never complained or felt bad that we would tease him about his English or would laugh at him. He would keep coming back for more ... and while we laughed, he learnt.

He would rarely get a spelling wrong more than once. And if he learnt something, he would immediately use that in a few sentences and make that word his very own.

His is an interesting story. He came to Mumbai from Amritsar because he wanted to dance. He was one of the best dancers in Punjab, saw no future for himself over there and came to Mumbai to make it big here in dancing.

He was still in the second year of his bachelor's degree when he got to Mumbai. While studying, he took up his passion for dance and started learning as much as he could from as many people who cared to teach him. Soon, he was teaching dance himself, albeit in an obscure studio in some godforsaken suburb. But it was a beginning.

He would visit the ashram frequently and stay with us, and each time he came, there would be some fresh thing he had learnt. Some new upgrade to his already phenomenal talent.

He watched me play the piano and asked me to teach him some stuff. I did. The next time he came back to ashram, he was playing what I had taught him brilliantly. I taught him more and pretty soon, he didn't need me. He was learning things naturally and organically by trusting his ear. I would still love for him to be trained by a good piano teacher. It would take his playing to another level. He already has a very good nice touch and feel for the music.

Then came singing. He learnt a bit from here and there, practised like a maniac and became quite good.

Good enough that he now performs in Raell Padamsee's *Broadway and Beyond*. Good enough that he has been dancing in *Grease* and other shows happening in Mumbai. He has already performed in most of Mumbai's classiest auditoriums, including St Andrew's and NCPA.

He continues to learn more dance styles and has slowly become more graceful every day.

Besides being a great learner, Chirag has that unmistakable flair for teaching. He can teach one on one and he can hold a crowd of a few thousand. His classes are exuberant and full of vitality. He quickly gauges how much you can do and somehow manages to make you do much more than what you thought.

Pretty soon, he saved enough money to get himself a second-hand car, and managed to afford the rent to live in a little apartment in Sion in Mumbai.

Till date, he has taught more than 10,000 students, choreographed and danced in many shows and ad promos and sang and danced in a plethora of stage productions in Mumbai.

He is a meditator and does Sudarshan Kriya regularly. He spends a lot of time with many people who smoke, drink and eat non-vegetarian food. Even so, he has managed to remain completely clean. That takes terrific belief in yourself and truckloads of self-confidence.

Chirag is going places for sure!

I could go on and on. I get so many mails from intelligent, smart people who say they can't get jobs or who are utterly fed up with their jobs and desperately want to do something else. These days, there are so many opportunities if you just care to look beyond 'getting a job'. Here is a quickie formula.

What are your passions? What do you absolutely enjoy doing? Make sure that these things are things you can do day in and day out. Don't make the mistake of confusing a hobby for a profession. For example, I enjoy playing the piano, but I would hate it if I had to practise eight hours a day. No way is music going to become my career. It's a hobby that I treasure and it will stay that way.

Once you have zeroed in on a few of your passions, start looking around you. Look at the place you live in; what is missing? What product or service are people looking for or complaining about? If your passion can be mapped to this missing element, bingo! You have a business idea.

Then it's all about belief in yourself and committed hard work.

If you are not getting a job, look around you. Assume you will NOT get a job. Now what will you do? Look for other opportunities. Hone other skills. I had an email from a guy saying that he had been looking for a job for the past eighteen months. In three months he could have learnt website programming and looked online for jobs people want done.

There is so much you can do to earn money if only you are open to the idea of stepping out from the conventional and trying your hand at something different. Google helps big time!

There is a Sanskrit shloka: *Udyoginaam, purushasimha, upayeti Laxmi.*

Laxmi (wealth and success) comes to the one who is willing to work diligently and has the courage of a lion. Believe that you have this courage and work hard. Keep your eyes wide open. When opportunity knocks, open the door.

THE REAL SECRET

There was quite a bit of a stir caused by a movie called *The Secret*. I must say it's a well-made movie. The message of the movie is the 'Law of Attraction' – Intention, Attention and Manifestation.

You think of stuff you want. You put a strong intention that it will happen for you in your life. You truly believe that you will get it – you visualize how nice your life will be when you have it, you make positive affirmations … and it will manifest for you.

This is a spin-off from an old Sanskrit proverb that was never a secret at all – *Yad Bhavam, Tad Bhavati*. As you feel (or think), so shall it happen. This sounds great, and amazingly, a few times it does work. Your mind is a pretty powerful little device you own.

यद् भावम् तद् भवति

However, there is a fatal flaw and a misinterpretation here.

Say your intention is that you are going to have pizza for dinner tonight. You sit there and visualize it in fantastic detail. 1080p. Maybe even 4K. How nice and thin the crust is, the perfect tanginess of the tomato sauce on it, the succulent mushrooms which are the toppings, the emerald green dots of the basil pesto, the perfectly baked golden brown melt-in-your-mouth mozzarella cheese, and the generous amount of extra virgin olive oil slathered on it… You can sit and think about how you will savour bite after bite of this piece of heaven.

But as long as you are only thinking about it, you are not going to get pizza for dinner. In fact, if you simply sit around and only visualize the pizza, chances are you are not going to get any dinner at all.

The intention part is fine. However, for the manifestation to happen, you will need to put your attention on action, instead of the intention. If you want that pizza, no amount of thinking about it is going to make it manifest ninety-nine times out of 100. A remote probability exists that a friend could drop in with exactly what you were visualizing. But this is serendipity and cannot really be relied on.

For you to have that pizza for dinner either you will have to cook it yourself, or get someone else to make it for you. For the manifestation to happen, you will need to focus your attention on the action of making it happen. To make stuff happen in your life, have an intention for sure. Then work hard to change that intention into reality.

Finally, be ready to wait for the manifestation.

Many people make the mistake of becoming too attached to the results of their actions. This is another road to hell.

Understand this: You only have control over your actions, never over the results of those actions.

For example, you plant a mango sapling. You have control over how deep you put it into the earth, over the quality and quantity of mud you use, the amount of fertilizer you put in, the amount of water you give it and when. You can even erect a little fence around it so a cow or a goat doesn't have a go at it.

Let's assume you did all this correctly and your little sapling is now a young tree ready to bear fruit. All that hard work is finally going to pay off in lovely delicious juicy mangoes. At this point, can you tell the tree to give you fifty big mangoes and thirty-five slightly smaller ones? Do you have any control over the number of mangoes the tree is going to bear? Not at all! You have to take what the tree gives.

Similarly, you have control over what you do or don't, as well as over all your actions and your inactions. You have no control whatsoever over the result; what you get because of those actions (or inactions). Hence, Indian sages from time immemorial have said, 'Don't bother about the result. Don't stress about it. It's anyway not in your hands.'

Intention, attention on action and non-attachment to the result of the action will lead to manifestation of the original intention in its own time.

After performing the action learn to wait. Know that whatever is yours will surely come to you. Know this and relax.

This is the secret of the secret.

There is more…

Almost everyone enjoys starting off on something new, and they have great enthusiasm and energy for the first few days. Then somehow things start going downhill. The energy peters out. The fire of the initial enthusiasm dwindles. An obstacle comes along and most people just give up. Ever wondered why this happens?

Most people don't think about why they want that new thing in their life in the first place. They never give a thought to why they are doing what they are doing.

Ganesh is quite overweight. A good friend gifts him a beautiful kurta on his birthday, but it is two sizes too small. Ganesh decides this is a sign that he should lose weight. He had always wanted to and this lovely kurta is the perfect reason to start doing something about it. It will be great to fit into it. He will look so nice!

He starts a diet plan, joins a gym and starts working out. He even manages to get through the initial pain his body feels, the pain we all feel when we go to the gym after a long break, when your body aches in places you never even knew existed.

He does this for two weeks. Frankly, he doesn't see much change. One day, while passing a sweet shop, he goes in, starts to indulge and says goodbye to the gym and the diet. He gifts the kurta off to another friend. He can always buy one more, right?!

Then he meets this girl. She is really nice. He feels she could be the one! After some initial pleasantries of getting to know each other, he is quite smitten. More importantly, she seems to be too. He asks her if she could consider him for something more than being a 'good friend'. She eyes him over and says, 'Come back after losing ten kilos.'

It's the gym and the diet again. She is really worth losing that belly. She is so full of laughter and fun and so pretty and so intelligent. This time he manages two months. But every time he would pass the sweet shop, thoughts would pop up out of nowhere in his head. Thoughts of gulab jamuns and jalebis, of mango barfi and sweet lassi, of kaju katli and shrikhand... Is any girl really worth giving all this up? If I actually manage to lose the weight, will I ever be able to eat all those amazing, luscious, yummy things? I know, I know, he thinks; a moment on the lips, a lifetime on the hips. But, oh! What a moment! Life needs to have more of these moments. Girls are like buses. One goes, another comes...

Bye bye gym, hello sweets!

Ahhhhhh ... heaven!

Later, at his office they have this yearly check-up. The doctor, after looking at his reports, bluntly tells him he is in the red. For continued existence on the planet, he will HAVE to lose weight. No sweets, just healthy food and lots of water. And exercise!

Now, no sweet shop holds sway over Ganesh. He eats healthy food, goes to the gym and in a year manages to shed off that extra weight. He is back in the green. Of course, he is feeling healthier and more confident. There is a bounce in his step. His belly doesn't jiggle when he walks. He did it!

What happened here?

Each time Ganesh set off to do exactly the same thing. Lose weight. The intention was clear. Yet he failed miserably the first two times and succeeded spectacularly the third time. What was the difference?

The reason.

The first two times the reason for losing weight was just not strong enough to overcome his cravings for sweets. So even though he was enthusiastic to begin with, the reason didn't have the power to sustain him till the end. The third time the reason was so strong that nothing could stop him from getting to where he wanted to be.

Intention ✓

Attention on Action ✓

Non-Attachment to Results ✓

Ability to Wait ✓

Even having all this doesn't guarantee manifestation because you give up on action without a strong enough reason for your original intention. Along with the four things listed above, you will need reasons strong enough to see you through any obstacle that might pop up. You need a super convincing answer to why you had that intention in the first place. Then you will never lose enthusiasm. If you have all this in place, ninety-nine times out of 100 you are guaranteed manifestation.

This is the real secret!

How about that one time? That's just bad luck!

Once, someone asked me, 'Does Gurudev (God) answer all our prayers?'

I said, 'Yes, absolutely. Only, sometimes the answer can be "No".'

WEALTH RULES

'They are filthy, stinking rich.' 'He has obscene amounts of money.' Many, many people use these kinds of adjectives to describe people who are affluent.

It's an unfortunate middle-class mentality to associate wealth with dirt or some transgressions of the law. Thinking that if someone is super rich, they must have done something wrong to amass that fortune is the loser's way to make themselves feel good about not being wealthy.

Many feel, 'I may not have so much money, but at least I have not done anything wrong. I have not hurt anyone. I have not broken any law. I have lived a clean life.' This absurd righteousness actually dooms them to a life of middle-class mediocrity or worse. They make it all right for themselves to not be wealthy. You will repel anything that you consider filthy or obscene. As long as you continue looking at wealth in this way, abundance will never come to you.

In Indian tradition, Goddess Laxmi symbolizes wealth, prosperity and abundance. If you wish to attract wealth, start by looking at wealth as a Goddess and give the Goddess her rightful place. Then you will start to attract abundance.

The old, old adage 'Save not where you must spend, spend not where you must save' is a great place to start understanding money. It's really common sense, but over the years, I have found that the trouble with common sense is that it's not quite as common as we think. It's simply amazing how people spend their money on things they absolutely don't need; buying things because they are on sale or because there is some freebie along with it.

I have seen people buy sub-standard washing powder because there is a bucket free along with it. They know the washing powder is not so nice. They know they don't need the bucket. Yet they buy.

The same people want discounts on really great products because they feel they cannot afford them. Everyone knows that having organic food is better than the usual genetically modified, pesticide and chemical-ridden junk that gets passed off as food these days. Having good wholesome organic food gives a tremendous boost to overall health and mental well-being of an individual. People will compromise on the vitality and quality of life of their loved ones just to save a few rupees. Big multiples of that same money go into health care later. This hidden cost that not only makes you poorer materially but can also cause much distress to body and mind is utterly neglected.

There are many such examples where you and I have been tricked into spending money in all the wrong places. Quality always comes at a price and it is always worth it. Spending money is as much an art as saving and investing it!

My parents had the habit of making envelopes and putting money in them. It was their way of budgeting their income.

These envelopes would be labelled with various headings – Electricity, Telephone, Entertainment, Vegetables, Milk, Wages for Servants, and so on. If, for example, the entertainment envelope had run out, there would be no movies or eating out for the rest of that month for us. Mom made sure that we never lived beyond our means and ingrained a sense of thriftiness in us. There was almost always moderation in everything we did.

One of the envelopes was labelled Emergency. Dad would always keep aside some money for emergencies – someone in the family falling ill, doctor's bills, medicines, stuff like that.

Somehow, illnesses plagued our home. My grandparents would keep falling ill. My mother would be sick on and off. My sister and I would have off days. Nothing happened to Dad. I think he was too busy keeping us all in good health to have the time to fall sick.

After I did the Art of Living series of courses, I asked Dad to throw away that envelope with Emergency written on it and replace it with another one with Family Vacations written on it. If there were an emergency, we would skip the vacation to take care of the emergency. Grudgingly he did it. Amazingly, the overall health of the entire family became so much better and we went for some really cool vacations!

Two lessons from this story:

Energy follows thought. Earn, save and invest money for good things, and chances are good things will happen to you.

Live within your means. I cannot stress this one enough. Don't ever spend more than you earn. It's a great feeling to be debt-free!

Martine taught me another valuable lesson about wealth.

Many years ago, I was in Paris and was staying with Martine in her beautiful apartment right in the middle of Paris, at St

Germain du Pres. Martine was an antique dealer specializing in chess sets and was quite well off. Her home was a tiny, tiny rooftop flat, but what it lacked in space it made up for by being utterly charming and really comfortable. She had a few exquisite pieces of art displayed around her lovely little home. Martine is now a dear, dear friend but at that time I hardly knew her and it was just my second or third time outside India.

Most evenings, Martine would take me for a walk. We were a stone's throw away from the River Seine and we would love to walk along the banks of the river, pausing here and there when we saw something interesting. I had great fun exploring the heart of Paris with her, eating at the little bakeries and pizzerias and generally admiring the architecture and gardens this enchanting, beautiful city had on display.

After a few days, I noticed Martine had a peculiar habit. Every time we left the house, she would put a coin or a small currency note into a fairly big glass bottle she kept by the side of her front door. Whenever we came back home she would do exactly the same thing again.

One evening, my curiosity got the better of me and I asked her about this strange custom she followed. She laughed and explained that she always felt enormously grateful and extremely lucky to lead the life she was leading. Every time she left home she put in a coin or two into the bottle to remind herself to feel thankful for the fantastic life she had, and every time she came back home, she

would put in a few more coins to remember to feel grateful for the beautiful space she had the privilege of coming back home to.

What did she do when the bottle was full? She donated it to a charity. She would pick a different one every time.

She said she would let me in on a secret. At that time, cat burglars who broke into homes, especially rooftop flats, plagued Paris. She had been burgled thrice already, but each time the burglar would make off with only the glass bottle. They would never touch her priceless antiques that were right there in plain sight! The money in the bottle was for charity anyway, she reasoned, and the thief was welcome to it.

One of the biggest secrets of attracting wealth is to donate a part of it to charity. When wealth is shared with people who are less fortunate, their blessings to you bring you even more money. Make sure you give a percentage of whatever you earn to those less fortunate than you are. Don't wait till you are earning 'lots' of money. Even if your only source of income is just the pocket money from your parents, make a habit of giving away a little bit from it. ten per cent of the profits out of the royalties of this book will be used to fund various Art of Living service projects.

The ability to give is the signature of being rich. Only a person who feels they have enough can share with others.

A few very obvious things you can do to create abundance:

1. Keep a specific place for wealth in your home. A safe or a locker in a cupboard works well. Keep that place neat and squeaky-clean. The Goddess will not make her home in a dirty place.

2. If you have a wallet or a purse to carry money, make sure it is not torn or damaged. You don't want to carry a Goddess in some stinky old wallet.

3. Don't leave loose change or currency notes all around the house. Have a bowl where people in the house can deposit that change. Our yearly vacations when we were kids used to get sponsored through our money bowl.

4. Be in the company of people who respect wealth. If people around you squander their money on meaningless things, you will have a tendency to do so too.

5. Never ever use derogatory words like filthy, stinking, obscene, etc., to describe prosperity.

6. Stinginess and amassing wealth doesn't work either. You cannot cage up the Goddess. You may be very rich, but you and the people around you will not be happy. And you will have missed the point of wealth. Wealth is never an end; it's always a means to an end.

One of the key differences between people who are rich and those who are not is that while rich people invest money, the others save money.

Saving money will never create more money. Given inflation and rates of interest in most banks, some fairly simple mathematics will reveal that if you save money, you are actually losing money and becoming poorer every year.

Investing money is far more intelligent. How to invest and where is totally beyond the scope of this book and my expertise. There are many books that will teach you how to do that and I encourage you to read them to learn how to grow your money.

A few possibly naïve words of caution:

Don't let greed overshadow your common sense. If something is too good to be true, it usually is. Don't get caught up in anything that promises quick money. It simply doesn't exist.

For those thinking of the share market, keep these two basic things in mind:

1. Never put into the share market what you are not willing to lose. It's typically a calculated gamble, but it is a gamble and you could lose.

2. My uncle once defined the share market for me. He said the share market is a device to take wealth from impatient people and give it to the patient ones. Time and compound interest are your biggest allies in the game of growing wealth.

If you consider that good health, love, education, the ability to meditate, fantastic friends, respect, a great upbringing, etc., are also contributors to your wealth, you will realize that you are much richer than you ever thought you were. Abundance begets abundance. Gratitude for all that you have and forbearance to wait and work for all that you want will make you very, very rich indeed.

Finally, check out the depiction of Goddess Laxmi as Illustration 10. She is shown seated in a lotus that is floating on water. This symbolizes that She is extremely whimsical and could sink any time! Wealth is like that. It can come and go.

Goddess Saraswati, the goddess of knowledge is portrayed seated on a rock in Illustration 11. This means that once you have acquired knowledge it will always be yours. So even if the capricious Goddess Laxmi abandons you for the time being, with the help of the steady Goddess Saraswati, you can easily win her back.

Just one more reason to study for knowledge!

MY INWARD JOURNEY

The journey from the head to the heart is just a few inches, but it is quite a journey!

I was giving my entrance exams for IIT. I had studied enough, knew most things I needed to know, but the morning of the exam, I had a terrible headache.

Dad had learnt some 'touch healing' spiritual thingy, but so far I had steered clear of it. That morning I thought, 'Why not?', and asked him to help relax me.

He did. And my headache and tiredness vanished, and I had a great exam, got into IIT for postgraduate studies in maths ... But more importantly, for a twenty-year-old who thought he knew everything, a certain faith in the Unknown and Unknowable was ignited.

I underwent a few courses and self-development seminars but always felt there was something missing, something not all there ... Until a good friend of mine bulldozed me into an Art of Living course.

(Phone rings)

Me: 'Hi!'

Shamal: 'Hey, what you doing over the weekend?'

Me: 'Nothing much really…'

Shamal: 'There is this course on breathing…'

Me: 'C'mon, Shamal, breathing is boring!'

Shamal: 'Look, I don't have time to talk to you; I have to call hundreds of other people. Just see to it that you are there or else…'

Me: 'OK, OK, will come… How much does it cost?'

Shamal: '*Tere ko kya farak padta hai, tera baap bharega!*'(What difference does it make to you, your father is going to pay for it!)

Me: 'Riiiight…'

And that was my introduction to the rest of my life. I didn't even know the name of the course I had enrolled for!

The Art of Living course was amazing. To experience a state of consciousness, a reality unlike any that I could even begin to dream about was a blessing and a gift. All my concepts of what I thought life was all about were shattered.

A serenity came that I never knew I had. Art of Living had given wings to my heart!

Very soon after my basic course, I went to Art of Living's Bengaluru ashram for my first advanced meditation course. Only when I reached the ashram did I get to know that the advanced course was a silence programme. I was the last one to leave the meditation hall that night the silence started and I think the last one to start speaking again when silence opened.

I was soaked in the bliss of me. What a wondrous thing to be able to do!

I was in love. And there was no going back. The Art of Living series of courses introduced me to me. That sparkling enchanting quiet space which all of us have within us.

These courses with their simple, powerful, profound techniques and scintillating knowledge about ourselves were Gurudev's (Sri Sri Ravi Shankar's) gift to the world.

I will not say that after the Art of Living courses, and even after becoming a teacher, that my problems went away and everything was always great. That I never got angry or never felt bad. Many times, life did suck. Problems did come, but along with them came the quiet confidence that I could handle them. I was simply amazed at how my inward journey so positively affected my outward expression and ability to deal with the challenges that life threw at me.

So began my journey from the head to the heart ... There were many adventures on the way and I am sure many more to come. This book has been about the adventure called learning and studying.

Meanwhile, if you have not yet embarked on this voyage inside of you, you have no idea what you are missing out on ... Nothing on this planet outside you can even begin to compare with what you have inside of you. Please do yourself a favour and learn to meditate. And if you already know how to meditate, see that you practise every day. It is a glorious thing to blossom, to love, to smile and to be able to spread those waves of positivity to others.

Gurudev is so very patient with me. Totally accepting of who I was and gently moving me to who I could be. It's one thing to force a rose open, it's quite another to give it the time it requires to blossom – that is what Art of Living and Gurudev have done for me and for countless others on the planet.

Thank you.

THE STORY OF YES!⁺

Afew moments spent with Gurudev can open doors to infinity for you, and for millions through you. A few words spoken by him can translate into your life story, and stories of millions through yours.

It was a special morning in the month of March of 2006 when Dinesh and I walked into Gurudev's kuteer in Rishikesh. He was meeting with the senior and experienced people in the organization and discussing with them what they would be doing for that year. To many, different roles and responsibilities were given. At the end of that meeting, when everyone had left, He took Dinesh and me aside and simply said, '*Tum log kuch youth ke liye karo*'(Both of you do something for the youth). And that was how YES!⁺ was born!

A nostalgic smile lights up my face as I recall those moments. That was it. Seven words. One instruction. 'Do something for the youth.'

Dinesh and I could have interpreted that as simply teaching a few Art of Living courses to young people in some colleges, but we took that instruction to its logical extreme and created a brand new course for youth! Many are grateful we did the latter.

Along with our team of super dynamic and dedicated teachers we started work on what came to be known as the 'YES!+' course. Youth Empowerment and Skills for people who are eighteen and above, which became Youth Empowerment and Skills for people for eighteen+ which finally evolved into YES!+.

Yup, that's what the '+' stands for.

We asked a lot of young people, students and young professionals that if a workshop were to be created for them, what would they want in it? We listened to their concerns and the challenges that they faced in their lives and the questions they wanted answered. We talked to people who were spiritual and to those who wouldn't touch spirituality with a barge pole. To youngsters who were successful and to the ones who had flunked. To those who were just starting out with jobs and to the ones striking out on their own with a fresh business idea. And who came from various different financial and social backgrounds. To young people aspiring to be doctors, architects, lawyers, engineers, actors, musicians, farmers, teachers, politicians…

We also took ourselves back to our college days and thought, 'When we were eighteen or twenty-two, what was happening in our life? What kind of a workshop would we have wanted to be on?'

And taking all those inputs, we came up with the contents of the course.

We took Gurudev's personal guidance on how we present and teach this very special course, what topics to include and what topics we shouldn't. We came up with many games and processes so that instead of us teaching anything, we would create situations so that our students would have realizations and those special wonderful 'a-ha!' moments. Very soon, we had designed a fabulous course and knew we were sitting on pure dynamite.

July 2006 saw the first YES!+ course of about 150 students taught by Dinesh and me in Mumbai. And then there was no looking back. It's been more than a decade now, and our team has grown to more than 1,000 YES!+ teachers in more than 120 countries. We have taught tens of thousands of young people the world over.

YES!+ has become a phenomenon and many of the leadership skills we required to take it to the next level are revealed in this book.

We promise to spread Gurudev's precious knowledge to more and more people across the globe in the time to come.

MIND MAPS AND THEIR ESSAYS

The Liver

How good is life?
It depends on the liver!

The liver is roughly a triangular-shaped organ sitting just below the diaphragm, extending across the width of the abdominal cavity. It's the biggest solid organ of the body, weighing around 1.5 kg. It is divided into the right lobe and the left lobe by the falciform ligament. The gall bladder is located alongside the right lobe and stores bile. The liver and gall bladder are connected to the intestine by the bile duct.

Some fun facts about the liver:

1. It can regenerate itself! If 87 per cent of the liver is cut off, it can still grow itself back to full size.
2. It holds 13 per cent of the body's blood supply at any given moment.
3. It filters one litre of blood every minute.

4. Has more than 500 functions, maintains over 2,000 internal enzyme systems and produces more than 13,000 chemicals.
5. The only organ to get blood from two supplies, the hepatic artery from the heart and the portal vein from the intestines. Blood leaves the liver through the hepatic veins.
6. The liver has no nerve endings, so you can't feel any pain there.

The liver makes blood proteins, clotting proteins, lipo proteins and 80 per cent of our cholesterol. It filters blood, makes bile, makes and breaks down hormones, regulates blood sugar and changes harmful toxins into substances that can be safely eliminated from the body. And this is just a quickie list of liver functions! If we lost the liver, we would die within twenty-four hours.

The liver basically processes anything and everything we eat or drink and either repackages it for the body to use or eliminates it. The liver detoxifies the body.

There are three major vital functions the liver is associated with:

1. **Purification**: The liver collects many toxins, transforms them to make them harmless and then eliminates them. It destroys old red and white blood cells as well as certain bacteria present in the blood. It destroys the toxins that come naturally from the waste products produced by our body (ammonia), as well as toxins that we may ingest (alcohol). It neutralizes the drugs we absorb after they have taken effect and prevents any dangerous accumulation.

2. **Synthesis**: It metabolizes carbohydrates, lipids (cholesterol and triglycerides) and proteins (albumen). It produces stuff that makes our blood clot and stops bleeding. It produces and secretes bile that is stored in the gall bladder.
3. **Storage**: It stores fat-soluble vitamins – A, D, K and E as well as glycogen. Energy is stored in the form of sugar, which it makes available to the body whenever required.

When things go wrong with the liver, the detoxification of the body stops, and all sorts of poisons start building up. Impurities build up in our bloodstream, our sugar metabolism levels are altered and our hormones that regulate energy levels and mood are affected. If the liver becomes toxic to the point where it is completely non-functional, drastic medical measures like a transplant are needed.

The most common diseases that affect the liver are hepatitis, fatty liver, cirrhosis and cancer. Most are reflection of our lifestyle and can be prevented fairly easily.

The three biggest favours you can do to your liver are:

1. Completely cut out alcohol, smoking or drugs from your life.
2. Exercise. Not just physical exercise like jogging, swimming and going to the gym, but also exercises to calm the body and mind, like yoga and meditation. Surya namaskars, Sudarshan Kriya and Sahaj Samadhi Meditation are highly recommended.
3. Sleep by midnight latest, preferably by 11.00 p.m. Ayurvedically speaking, the liver heals and detoxes itself between 10.00 p.m. and 2.00 a.m. If you are resting at this

time, chances of problems with the liver are reduced to virtually nil.

Eating good food will go a long way in helping the liver do its job.

1. Dark green leafy vegetables and orange, yellow, purple and red coloured fruits support the liver.
2. Bitter foods, romaine lettuce, broccoli, dill, caraway seeds, garlic, turmeric, onion and cayenne give big boosts to the liver.
3. Asparagus, avocado, watermelon and mushrooms have antioxidants that help the liver (and the rest of the body).
4. Fruit and veggie juices help cleanse the liver.
5. Warm water with lemon every day alkalizes the system.
6. Chlorophyll can protect you from carcinogens like no other food or medicine. It detoxifies the liver and cleanses and adds oxygen to the bloodstream, which is critical for optimal liver function. A superb source of chlorophyll is chlorella.
7. Avoid or eliminate eating roadside food where the water is questionable.

The liver is a super hard worker and is fundamental to good health and a great life. Take care of the liver and it will take care of you! Illustration 18 depicts the liver mind map.

The Mojito

The Mojito (pronounced Mo-Hee-Toh) is considered to be one of the oldest cocktails of Cuba.

It has a disputed history. Some say it was created at the time when Sir Francis Drake landed in the city of Havana. An associate of his called Richard Drake created an early version called El Draque using lime, sugar, mint and aguardiente (a sort of rum).

Others say that African slaves working in the sugar fields of Cuba made it. The word mojito stems from the African word mojo, which means to place a little spell. Ernest Hemingway became a fan of the drink and it rose to international prominence.

Whatever the origin, the combination of lime and mint is going to stick around for a long time.

Here is my favourite recipe of the non-alcoholic version of the mojito; according to me, it does cast a mojo on whoever drinks it!

You will need:

A lime cut into thin wedges, we use 2-3 wedges for each drink
6-7 fresh mint leaves
½ a glass of sugarcane juice
A few glugs of sparkling water (soda)
3-4 ice cubes

You will need to chill the glass you are going to make the mojito in, so leave the glass in the freezer for ten minutes or so. Finally, you will need a muddler and a cocktail shaker. A muddler is an unvarnished long (20-30 cms) wooden stick with a rounded bottom.

Put the mint leaves and the lime wedges into a cocktail shaker. Muddle with circular motion. To muddle means to crush (using the muddler) the mint and the wedges until both release some juice. It takes just a few seconds to do this.

Add the sugarcane juice and ice to the cocktail shaker and close the lid. Shake a few times, around 10-15 seconds. Transfer everything to the chilled glass. Top up with just a few glugs of the sparkling water and stir the drink.

Garnish with a lemon rounder and some mint leaves. Drink right away.

For a typically Indian taste, you can add a few pinches of jaljeera powder to your drink. I call that the Jaljeera Mojito.

Mint, when muddled, can help cure stomach aches and relieve chest pain. Lemon lowers the pH of the drink and has vitamin C. Lemon peel neutralizes free radicals. Sugarcane juice has a lot of proteins, some carbohydrates and traces of calcium, iron, potassium and sodium. Sparkling water can help ease symptoms of indigestion. Jaljeera is fantastic for digestion.

It does cast a little spell on body and mind, does it not? Enjoy it with people you love. See Illustration 19 for the complete mind map of this delicious drink!

The Sun

The Sun, the centre of our solar system, is a star. This means it has no solid surface. Just hydrogen (92.1 per cent) and helium (7.8 per cent), all held together by its own gravity.

Our Earth is pretty big. The circumference of the Earth at the equator is around 40,000 km. The Earth weighs in at a hefty 5.97×10^{24} kg.

Jupiter, one of our neighbouring planets, is much, much bigger. Around 317 Earths could fit into it! It weighs 1.89

$\times 10^{24}$ kg. There are many other planets in our solar system, some huge, some quite small. There are thousands, perhaps millions of comets and asteroids. Even so, the Sun is super, super, super, (I could go on, but you get the idea) huge compared to all the planets, asteroids, comets and anything else there might be in our solar system. So big that more than a million Earths could fit in the Sun. It actually makes up 99.86 per cent of the mass of the entire solar system! The rest of the solar system seems to be negligible compared to the Sun … you, me, our friends and families, our homes, our cities, our Earth, the moon and all the other stuff in the solar system hardly matters!

The Sun is the closest star to Earth, just 149.6 million km away. It is also the most perfect sphere observable in nature.

Our ancestors built many rocks and carvings that tracked the passage of the Sun and the moon. Even in the very primitive times, man had realized the life-giving nature of the Sun. The interaction between the Sun and the Earth drive the weather, the tides and the seasons on Earth.

Without the intense heat of the Sun, no life on Earth would have been possible. The temperature at the Sun's core is 15 million degrees Celsius. (That's quite a bit hotter than even Chennai in May.)The thermonuclear reactions that happen in the core of the Sun produce most of the light and heat we get here on Earth.

The Sun's immense gravity squeezes hydrogen atoms. As the pressure and heat rise, there are nuclear fusion reactions that cause the hydrogen atoms to crash together. They combine to form heavier atoms like helium. This process gives the heat that rises and blooms to the surface of the Sun. It doesn't seem like much when you read this but one would need to explode 100 billion tons of dynamite every second to match the energy created at the core of the Sun.

The energy from the core takes 1,70,0000 years to get to the Sun's surface, which is around 500 km thick. The surface is quite cool at just 5,500 °C (Still much hotter than Chennai in May). The radiation escapes the Sun's surface and we see that as light here on Earth around eight minutes afterwards.

The Sun and its atmosphere are divided into several zones and layers. The solar interior, from the inside out, is made up of the core, the radiative zone and the convective zone. The solar atmosphere above that consists of the photosphere, the chromosphere, the transition region and the corona. Beyond that is the solar wind, an outflow of gas from the corona.

The magnetic field of the Sun is just two times stronger than the Earth's own field. Unlike the Earth's magnetic field, which has a single north and south pole, the Sun has a writhing, chaotic mass of magnetic fields all twisting and churning against each other. This happens because the Sun is all gas and it rotates in a very weird way. The insides rotate faster than the surface and the parts at the equator spin faster than those at higher latitudes. This creates kinks and twists in the magnetic field, which result in the magnetic field becoming up to 3,000 times stronger than the Earth's at some points. These crazy distortions cause the sunspots, the flares, the prominences and the coronal ejections.

Sunspots are relatively cool, dark features on the Sun's surface, often roughly circular, caused when dense magnetic lines break through to the Sun's surface. They have a cycle of around eleven years.

A prominence is an arc of gas that erupts from the surface of the Sun and can go hundreds and thousands of kilometres into space after which it loops back down to the surface. It can stay and remain visible for months.

The flares are the most violent eruptions in the entire solar system, and a single coronal mass ejection can spew out a balloon of twenty billion tons of matter!

These magnetic storms have an effect on Earth as well ... sometimes overloading and outright burning power stations and power lines on the surface of the Earth, many times enhancing the ethereal dazzling display of Northern and Southern lights – the aurora borealis and the aurora australis. They can also degrade GPS and damage satellites in high orbits.

The ancients of India revered the Sun and created a set of yogic asanas known as the surya namaskars, which are perhaps the most complete set of exercises I know of. They exercise literally every part of the body. The light of the Sun in the early morning and evening is said to have a very beneficial effect on human beings, and these are perfect times to enjoy a walk outside.

Our Sun, like any energy source, is not forever. It is middle-aged, around 4.5 billion years old, and right now is classified as a yellow dwarf star. It is expected to live for approximately another five billion years ... and by that time, it will have used up all its hydrogen and start to burn helium. This will cause the Sun to expand to about 100 times its current size, swallowing Earth and many other planets. It will become a red giant and burn for another billion years or so, after which it will collapse into a white dwarf, a star about the size of the Earth.

Hopefully, we could have perfected space travel well before this time and will be able to see the entire show from a safe vantage point. See Illustration 16 for the complete mind map.

Why Are Mirror Neurons Exciting?

The adult human brain contains approximately 100 billion neurons. Each of these can grow 1,000 to 10,000 fibres called dendrites and interact with each other through them. The number of interactions that can happen through the permutations and combinations of the dendrites is truly humungous. So big that it is postulated to be bigger than the number of elementary particles in the universe!

The neurons in the frontal part of the brain fire whenever you do something. There is a set of neurons, for example, which will fire when you reach out and pick a mango. Another set which will fire when you pick your nose and so on. These are called command neurons. They command the body to do certain things.

There is a very fascinating subset of neurons in the frontals. Around 20 per cent of the neurons in the frontals are called mirror neurons. These were discovered accidentally while performing some tests on monkeys. While the command neurons in the monkey were firing while it was doing some action; a set of neurons were firing in another monkey watching the first monkey do that action. This finding was then confirmed in human beings as well.

If you see me eat a very bitter fruit and make a face, don't you almost experience it yourself? You too cringe inwardly and empathize with me. This is caused by mirror neurons.

This single discovery could shed more clarity on our evolution as a species, why some children are autistic and what could be done to help them, the Sanskrit shloka '*Aham Brahmasmi*', 'You are (the) One' (or, freely translated, we are all One), that forms the basis of Indian spirituality and what makes a great comic among many other things.

Our brains developed to their present size and sophistication 2,00,0000 years ago. However, we as a species really exploded on the planet just 40,000 years ago. Somehow, the mirror neurons in all of us got triggered. This meant that we didn't have to wait for evolution's long slow march to grant us knowledge we would need to survive as a species. We got it simply from watching each other and learning from each other. This spread horizontally through the human race and vertically downwards to all our children, making each generation smarter and smarter through simple observation and imitation!

Autistic children don't learn from their environment as normal children do. This retards their growth. Could it be that because of some mutation their mirror neurons don't fire? And so could some repair work be done there to make sure they do? This could be a cure for autism and such a hope and a blessing for so many children and their families.

When you watch someone squeeze someone else's hand, your mirror neurons are firing. The only reason you don't feel the sensation yourself is because there are sensory cells in your hand giving information to the brain that no one is touching you. So you can 'empathize' but not actually feel. Your skin prevents you from getting muddled. But in case your hand is an esthetized, meaning your sensory cells are put out of commission, and you see someone squeezing someone else's

10 Goddess Lakshmi

11 Goddess Saraswati

	most alkaline	moderately alkaline	least alkaline
fruits	 lemon, watermelon dried dates/figs, kiwi mango, papaya, pear grapes, pineapple	apple, avocado banana, orange apricot, guava gooseberry	cherry, coconut ripe olive
veggies	asparagus, capsicum	carrot, celery, bean lettuce, bell pepper peas, broccoli, turnip ginger, garlic, cabbage pumpkin, potato + skin	tomato, fresh corn mushroom, onion, lee cucumber, sprout eggplant, water chest
nuts			almond, chestnut sesame seed
grains			amaranth, millet quinoa
dairy		 ghee	
other	herb teas	green tea, apple cider vinegar	olive oil, soy product flax seed oil, pickles sea salt
	most alkaline	*moderately alkaline*	*least alkaline*

plum, berries
prune

green banana

cooked spinach
dry beans

skinless potato

nutmeg, pistachio
sunflower/pumpkin
seeds, cashew, walnut
macadamia

peanut

cornmeal, rye, bran
barley

breads (rye, oat, corn
rice), buckwheat
whole wheat/whole grain
brown/basmati rice

wheat/white flour
foods- pastries, pasta
white rice

tter (fresh/unsalted)
esh cream, yoghurt
ow whey, cow milk

milk (homogenised)
salted butter, goat milk
buttermilk, cheese

pasteurised honey,
maple syrup

ketchup, soy sauce

black tea. soft drinks
coffee, white vinegar
table salt, sugar

neutral | least
acidic | moderately
acidic | most
acidic

COULD A CURE BE PRESENT SIMPLY BY WORKING ON MIRROR NEURONS?

AUTISM IS INABILITY TO LEARN THROUGH OBSERVATION OF ENVIRONMENT

COULD UNDER DEVELOPED MIRROR NEURONS BE THE CAUSE?

REMOVE SKIN AND WE ARE ALL ONE!

MIRROR NEURONS ALLOW YOU TO EMPATHISE, BUT NOT ACTUALLY FEEL BECAUSE OF SENSORY CELLS IN YOUR SKIN

Thanks

THANKS TO MIRROR NEURONS FOR ALL THE LAUGHTER

LOTS OF COMED

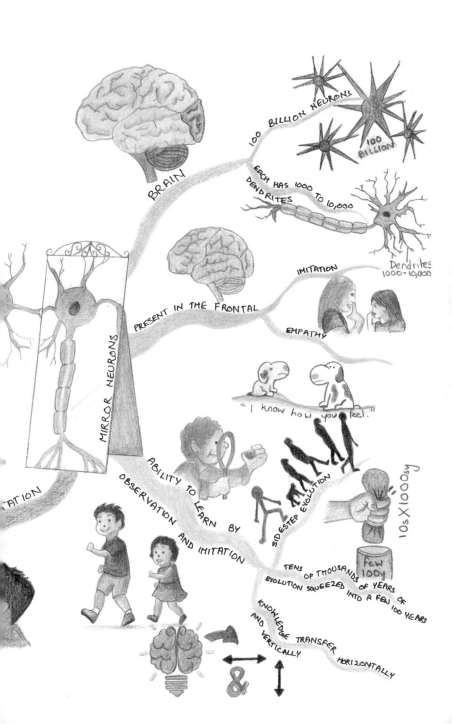

Prana

The warmth you feel
When you watch the rising sun,
Or the coolness,
when you see a loved one return.

Or the thrill,
When you do the forbidden...
Or the rush
When you find something hidden.

Or the buzz
While engaging in the monumental,
Or the tightness,
When someone is kind and gentle.

Or the flutter
When your crush smiles at you
Or the gush
When a baby keeps hugging you.

Or the rouse
When the cold water hits you,
Or the surge
When sitting next to the Guru.

All of these are
Expressions of the prana,
Found even, in
All flora and fauna.

When this Prana goes low
Even a friend appears a foe...
And in life, we stagger and fall,
As if we've had too much alcohol.

The question then remains
How to trigger Prana gains...
Any tips or tricks to boost it?
Will explain... if you permit.

Happy food, and sleep of the happy kind,
Happy breaths and a calm meditative mind...
Can drive away stubborn lethargy
And raise the subtle life force energy.

Source number one is food...
It even affects your mood.
What you eat, and when you eat,
And in 'How', and 'how much' you cheat.

Gorging late in anger or depression,
Can increase that emotion,
and bring on exhaustion.
Eating happy, fresh, natural and light...
Balances Rajas and Tamas,
Gives Sattvic might!

Daily between any meals two,
Let more than 3 hours pass through...
On moon's eleventh day – Ekadashi,
Drink lots of water, and go foodfree.

Today, Eating Meat is so not neat...
Your body and animals you mistreat.
The land and water for that you need
Can 30 times more vegetarians feed!
Not good for your energy or emotions,
The ecology or economy of nations.

Such subtle energy and a welcome relief...
Sleep heals, and soothes, even if it's brief.
With the Divine on the mind
Sleep is meditative and refined...
On a firm bed and No North head,
In Shavasan, do happily drop dead.

The difference between life and death,
What a mystery is our darling breath!
While the incoming energizes...
The outgoing detoxes and relaxes.

The breath, Left or right, long or short,
Is a guiding friend and constant consort.
Every rhythm has its own effect,
Enjoy the breath, with love and respect.

Another eternal source of our Prana,
Other than the breath's aana paana...
Is the mind, Meditative and happy,
In contrast to scattered, and snappy.

A scattered mind energy dissipates
A focused one, like a laser radiates.
Any task done cribbing and resisting
Will drain us out, and induce quitting.
Working with focus, and joyful willingness,
Perks us up, and creates winningness!

Thus the Prana's four sources
Learnt On Art of Living courses,
Enliven us, and make us surrender...
To life's beauty, love, and wonder!!

PS-High Prana, even makes you study better!
– Dinesh

All About Me

I am the Body, some say just a dream...
I serve to express, but try to impress.
I am made of the food I chew,
Shaped by the exercise I do.
Pure and strong I should be,
But is there all there is to me?

I am the flow, I am the Breath,
My in and out, is birth and death.
I connect the body with the mind
My rhythms can recharge, or unwind.
Controlling me, life's game is won!
I can be cool, I can be fun!

I am the Mind, an energy field
With thoughts and feelings, I am rewarded.
Past and future I instantly traverse,
In the present moment, joyfully immense.
The world I enjoy through the five senses
Gaining strength, when I drop my defenses.

I am the Intellect, called upon to decide,
To go for the good, or with the bad abide.
Judgements and doubts are my disease,
Boosts of prana, my welcome release.
Innocence triggers my intuition,
Beyond my scope, lies the Mystery of Creation!

I am the Memory, storing past impressions,
With it, I can force current expressions.
Clinging to the negative
Can become quite addictive,
But meditation and grace make me free,
Forgive the past, erase unwanted history

I am the Ego, subtle and powerful,
Entertaining and at times frightful.
To complicate and divide is my rule,
My biggest fear, is to be a fool.
But Naturalness humbles me,
Unconditional love tumbles me.

Am I all of the above, or above it all?
Who is wondering deep, who is watching tall.
The eye of the eye of the mind of the mind,
The infinite eternal spirit, One of its kind.
Am I the truth, or the love beyond emotion?
Am I the wave, or the whole of the ocean?
Am I the empty space that was and will ever be?
I know, and yet I don't,
Who or What is the real Me!

— Dinesh

19

EASES STOMACH ACHE

pain

RELIEVES CHEST PAIN

MINT WHEN MUDDLED

pain

pH LOWERS PH OF JUICE AND MAKES IT ANTI BACTERIAL

VITAMIN C

LEMON

LEMON PEEL NEUTRALIZES FREE RADICLES

Ca CALCIUM TRACE METALS SUGAR CANE JUICE

Fe IRON

K POTASSIUM

PROTEINS

SODIUM CARBS

Na SPARKLING WATER

EASES SYMPTOMS OF INDIGESTION

JALTEERA

FANTASTIC FOR DIGESTION

HEALTH BENEFITS

VERY OLD COCKTAIL FROM CUBA CIRCA 1500

ATTRIBUTED TO EITHER RICHARD DRAKE OR AFRICAN SLAVES

HISTORY

MOJO, AN AFRICAN WORD MEANS TO CAST A LITTLE SPELL

ERNEST HEMMINGWAY LOVED IT AND IT GOT INTERNATIONAL RECOGNITION CIRCA 1800

THE OLD MAN AND THE SEA

ERNEST HEMINGWAY

INGREDIENTS

7-8 MINT LEAVES

1/2 GLASS SUGARCANE JUICE

2-3 LEMON WEDGES

4-5 ICE CUBES

A FEW GLUGS OF SPARKLING WATER

(OPTIONAL) A FEW PINCHES OF JALJEERA

SERVE IN A CHILLED TALL GLASS

MUDDLING

MUDDLER: VARNISHED 20-30cm WOODEN STICK WITH ROUNDED BOTTOM

MUDDLING - USING A MUDDLER TO GENTLY CRUSH INGREDIENTS IN A CIRCULAR MOTION

PROCESS

MUDDLE 5 MINT LEAVES & LEMON WEDGES - IN A COCKTAIL SHAKER

ADD ICE & SUGARCANE JUICE & SHAKE IT UP

STIR IN FEW GLUGS OF SPARKLING WATER & OPTIONALLY JALJEERA

TRANFER EVERYTHING TO THE - CHILLED GLASS

GARNISH WITH A LEMON ROUNDER - AND FEW MINT LEAVES

Jal Jeera masala

MOJITO
(pronounced
Mo-hee-toh)

hand, chances are you WILL feel that sensation on your own hand! These are your mirror neurons at work. This can lead to the confirmation of the tenet of Indian spirituality that says we are all one. We are indeed all one. Just skin separates us. There are huge groups of neurons talking to each other all the time!

Finally, a lot of comedy is in imitation. We love watching people imitate other people. Could great comedians have fabulous mirror neurons? Can we credit mirror neurons for much of the laughter and happiness the world over since time immemorial?

There is no doubt about it. Mirror neurons are pretty exciting! (See Illustration 13.)

Stories about Shivaji

'You hide away in the hills like a monkey!' taunted a Mughal to Shivaji.

'Yes, but remember it was the monkeys who destroyed Ravana and his mighty army,' was Shivaji's reply.

Shivaji was born in the fort of Shivaneri in 1627 and named Shiva after the local Goddess Shivai.

When he was just ten years old, Shahaji, his father, took the little boy to pay his respects to Sultan Adilshah of Bijapur. Shahaji and the other courtiers prostrated themselves, touching their turbans to the floor. Shivaji refused to do this. He greeted the sultan with the *Maratha Salaam*, a simple manly gesture that he had seen his people do when they greeted their superiors. His 'obstinate defiance' would have earned him severe punishment had it not been for the high favour that his father enjoyed in the court of the sultan.

And so the stage was set. Here was a hero in the making. From his mother Jijabai he learnt the fierce pride in his culture and traditions and swore to protect them with his entire being and revive the Hindu way of life in India.

Till the age of fifteen, he mixed and mingled freely with absolutely everyone. He didn't see caste or creed. He played in the mountain and valleys and forests with his friends until he knew the topology inside out. He was, infact, meticulously building his army and his spy network and familiarizing himself with the local terrain.

At around fifteen he started with open defiance. His first real fight happened at Purandar Fort. His rag-tag army of a few hundred was going to face the organized might of a Mughal army of a few thousands, that too without weapons!

His strategy was masterly. A small group of his men would routinely harass the enemy. Just a quick sortie in and out of their camp, until they grew weary. They never knew if the war had started or not. The badgering had its desired effect. The Mughals attacked the fort. They were beaten by rolling stones. The defence of the fort was almost purely topological. Boulders were strategically placed and rained down on the invading soldiers. The hapless Mughals literally didn't know what hit them. Three waves were vanquished and their numbers whittled down. Then Shivaji and his bunch of invigorated fighters came out in full force to beat the fatigued Mughals. It was a rousing victory!

At Pune, Shahaji got the Lal Mahal built, and from there the young prince started his career. The Torna, Kondana and Rajgad forts fell to his growing might.

One of his secrets was that he had the common people with him. No woman or child was ever harmed by anyone in his army. The penalty for anyone doing that was that their hands and legs were cut off. No village was looted. If supplies were needed for his army, they would have to be purchased from the villagers. Even which trees could be cut for firewood was prescribed. Trees like mango or coconut were to be left as they were. Only trees like babool could be cut.

He fostered courage and fearlessness in his troops, inspiring them to perform humanly impossible feats on the battlefields.

From a paltry few hundred soldiers inherited from his father, over the years Shivaji created an army of over a hundred thousand. Many times, he would spot someone very ordinary with an extraordinary talent and through his charisma recruit that person to his cause. A few times, even his enemies would join him because of the aura of righteousness and valour he carried.

Bajiprabhu Deshpande was once Shivaji's enemy. But Shivaji won him over to his cause.

Every child in Maharashtra knows the story of Bajiprabhu Deshpande even now. Shivaji was making his escape from the Mughals and had to pass through a narrow path to freedom. Unfortunately, his cover had been blown and the enemy was hot in pursuit. Bajiprabhu Deshpande and a handful of his men promised Shivaji that they would hold the pass until they got the signal that he had reached safety.

A few people stood at that pass that day and held off a few thousand for more than six hours. Every single one of them died, but their king had reached sanctuary. It is said that Bajiprabhu was so spectacularly ferocious while fighting on that fateful day that he was invincible even when attacked by twenty to thirty men. To stop him, he had to be shot by arrows and his head was cut off. It is said that even then, to the horror of his enemies, his headless body continued to fight. Only the signal that Shivaji had reached his destination sucked the life from this great warrior.

Shivaji was a great administrator. During peacetime, all his soldiers would be engaged in creating infrastructure. Roads, bridges, dams and canals would be made to make the life of the common people better. He had part-time soldiers-farmers who tended the fields eight months in a year and fought for him the rest of the time. They were paid for their time. He introduced a cabinet of sorts to take care of administrative policies and justice. He had a central intelligence department. He militarized entire sections of society, across all classes, with the peasant populations near forts actively involved in the defence of the forts.

Though Shivaji was a devout Hindu, he had tolerance for other religions in his kingdom. He allowed freedom of religion in his subjects and opposed forced conversions.

His astonishing inclusivity can be seen in a letter he wrote to Aurangzeb –

'Verily, Islam and Hinduism are terms of contrast. They are used by the true Divine Painter for blending the colours and filling in the outlines. If it is a mosque, the call to prayer is chanted in remembrance of Him. If it is a temple, the bells are rung in yearning for Him alone.'

Shivaji had several Muslims in his army and navy.

The missionaries of Christianity were also never attacked.

There is a wonderful story of Shivaji and Saint Ramdas. Shivaji was around thirty years old, war-weary and tired. He met Saint Ramdas and was totally taken in by the peace and love that the saint radiated.

The boy, who had not bowed down before the sultan, immediately prostrated to the saint and surrendered his kingdom to him. Ramdas accepted the gift and told Shivaji to continue ruling on his behalf. After this incident it is said Shivaji never felt the burden of being a king.

Shivaji sacked the rich Mughal port of Surat and provoked an organized attack from the centre. He was resolutely beaten and went to Agra to negotiate.

Shivaji and his son Sambhaji were prisoners of Aurangzeb in Agra along with a huge contingent of Shivaji's soldiers. Aurangzeb was planning to send Shivaji and his men off to fight at the frontiers.

Shivaji feigned severe illness and requested to send his troops back to the Deccan, thereby ensuring their safety. He then requested to send daily shipment of gifts and sweets to the holy men and temples of the city as offerings to recover his health. This continued for several days. In the beginning, everything leaving his apartments would be meticulously checked, but as time went by, the security grew lax. Shambhaji was a child and had no restrictions. He went out of the prison camp. Shivaji disguised himself as one of the labourers who would carry the gifts out of the apartments and escaped. Shivaji and Shambhaji fled back to the Deccan disguised as sadhus. Shivaji himself spread news about the death of Shambhaji to deceive the Mughals and protect the child.

Then, like a veritable phoenix rising from the ashes, within a short span, with concerted attacks on the Mughal garrisons, Shivaji regained most of his lost territory.

He created a fantastic navy to guard the Konkan coast against invaders and is rightly called the father of the Indian Navy.

Shivaji was formally crowned 'Chattrapati' at the Rajgad Fort in 1674. He died in 1680 at Rajgad. Shivaji is remembered as an icon of freedom because of his struggle against a tyrannical and despotic imperial army. Two centuries later, he was one of the inspirations for the Indian freedom struggle from the British Raj. He was a wise and just king, a brilliant tactician, a fantastic administrator, a visionary with the ability to inspire others to dream his dream and fight for it. His rule is considered to be one of the golden ages of India. See Illustration 17 for the complete Shivaji mind map.

You may download high resolution images of these mindmaps from our website: http://www.bawandinesh.in/ books/readystudygo/downloads/mindmaps

It took us a little over three years to make our board game called Mumbai Connection. You can check it out on http:// www.mumbaiconnection.in

Using conscious and subconscious states of mind to ideate and create, and almost all other techniques discussed in this book we came up one of the first seriously fun board games of India, Mumbai Connection.

The rules may seem overwhelming and complicated, but a little effort to familiarise yourself with them and two or three games later, you will see their inherent simplicity and get totally hooked.

Mumbai Connection is wholesome family entertainment. A fantastic way to engage the rational and the emotional parts of the brain, to connect with friends and family, fight, argue, win and lose. Four players (or teams of players) tempt luck, tackle naughty and devious characters, celebrate or endure Mumbai city events, enhance their financial planning, organising skills, critical thinking and problem-solving in this colourful, captivating fun game about the complex rail network of one of the most happening cities in the world.

As a challenge, see if you can mind map the rule book of Mumbai Connection. If you manage to do it, consider yourself a champion mind mapper!

You can download the manual from http://www.mumbaiconnection.in/binder1.pdf

THE RECIPES

The internet is bursting with recipes of all sorts for all types of tastes and whatever level of healthiness you could care for.

Cooking is alchemy. It is almost magical how two or more ingredients that taste pretty awful by themselves produce an absolutely enchanting flavour when combined. A foray into the kitchen can be quite an adventure, and one can never be sure what treasures one will come away with…

Here are a few of my favourite recipes and a few from my friends. These are fairly basic and quick to make. They act as a base for more complicated stuff that you could dream up for yourself. They are mostly healthy and very tasty!

D.I.Y. Smoothie

Choose one of the following:
   Yogurt
   Coconut water
   Milk (less fat the better, desi organic cow's milk is best)

Choose two or three of:

Peaches (2)

Bananas (2)

Strawberries (7-8)

Mixed frozen berries (a generous handful)

Mango (1-2)

Papaya (7-8 chunks)

Pineapple (7-8 chunks)

Spinach (small bunch, baby spinach is better)

Make sure if washing is required, it's washed well before using it.

Flavour with one or two of the following:

Vanilla

Chocolate

Cinnamon powder

Lemon

Definitely add 1-2 spoons of one of the following:

Oats

Granola

Flax seed powder

Crushed almonds

Optionally add a spoon of one of the following:

Peanut butter

Almond butter

For sweetening:

You may add organic honey, raisins, raisin syrup or any natural sweetener.

Absolutely no sugar or any artificial sweetener.
Don't forget a few ice cubes to chill it.
Blend and drink ice cold, first thing in the morning!

Gowrishankar's Power Shake

Yes. It's the same Gowrishankar who gave us the rasam recipe in the mind mapping chapter. One day, I was feeling drained and super thirsty, and I asked him to make me something really nice. He made me this concoction with whatever happened to be there in the kitchen and it was so energizing and tasty, I have had him make it over and over again for me. This is the first time this recipe is being shared!

You need a powerful mixie to handle this. We use a Vitamix.

Chill two big mugs in the fridge while you get the other stuff together.

Put:
1 juicy apple, cut into chunks,
1 medium-sized preferably desi (red) carrot, peeled and cut into chunks,
1 inch ginger, peeled and grated,
½ tsp cinnamon powder,
2-3 leaves of fresh mint,
4 leaves of fresh basil,
1 tbsp of rose syrup (more if you want it sweeter),
2 cups of cold water and a few pieces of ice

into your blender jar, and add the juice of 4-5 tangerines or oranges and the juice of one lemon. Whir for a few minutes until completely blended. Pour into the mugs and enjoy chilled!

You may skip the rose syrup if you don't want the sugar. It still tastes amazing as long as the fruits are ripe, sweet and juicy. Feel free to add other fruits and see what happens.

Ankita's Sprout Salad:

For the sprouts:

Take one bowl each of Bengal gram (kala chana) and green moong, wash them well and soak them overnight in water. Water should be triple the quantity of sprouts in the vessel.

Next morning, put the legumes in a wet muslin cloth and tie it tightly and hang it. After another twenty-four hours sprouts will be ready.

Steam the sprouts for 7-10 minutes. Let them cool.

Dry roast equal quantities of cumin (jeera) and fenugreek (methi) seeds on a skillet over low heat for about ten minutes. Grind to a powder in a mixie. I make quite a bit of it and store this powder in an airtight bottle.

For the Salad:

Finely/thinly chop the following:

      1 big juicy apple, unpeeled
      1 tangerine (remove the skin and seeds)
      1 or two pomegranates
      2 tomatoes, after peeling their skins
      1 carrot
      A handful of baby spinach leaves
      A few green grapes, deseeded

A small bunch of coriander leaves

5-8 big leaves of fresh basil

Add to this mixture:

1 tsp of jeera and methi roasted powder

1 tsp chaat masala

1 tsp cinnamon powder

1 tbsp maple syrup

Juice of 1/2 a lemon

Add in the sprouts.

Optionally add one tbsp each of pinenuts, watermelon seeds and sunflower seeds.

Toss thoroughly.

Garnish with chopped coriander.

Keep the mixture in the fridge for about an hour to chill. Serve cold. Eat fresh.

You may add seasonal fruits like pineapple, pear, raw mango, etc., to this according to your taste.

The sprouts are high in fibre and proteins and have a low glycaemic index. They help the body lose weight and are a great source of iron. Free radicals in them can protect you from harsh sunrays and prevent skin cancer. They prevent anaemia, boost immunity, stabilize blood sugar levels and helps maintain healthy blood pressure.

The different coloured fruits and greens provide all vitamins (A, B, C, E) and essential minerals and antioxidants. They are rich in fibre and water content.

The mixture of roasted jeera and methi seeds is good for combating acidity.

This salad is truly a holistic, healthy and surprisingly tasty package!

Fresh Green Leafy Salad

Gather:

A small bunch each of:

Argula or rocket leaves

Lettuce leaves of all sorts – green, romaine, butterhead, etc.

Baby beet greens

Baby spinach leaves

Any other green leaves you care for. It doesn't matter if some are not available, but it's great to have at least three varieties.

10 baby tomatoes

2 small sweet carrots, diced into small cubes or julienned

½ red and yellow bell pepper, chopped small

1 tbsp pine nuts, sunflower seeds, watermelon seeds

½ cup of fresh feta cheese, crumbled

Wash the salad leaves well and dry them. Add all the above ingredients together into a big salad bowl. Chill in the fridge for about an hour.

The simplest and tastiest salad dressing I know is to take a few glugs of olive oil and add to that the juice of one lemon and a dash of salt and pepper. Shake this really well.

If you want to get fancier with your dressing, add one or more of the following:

1 tsp of brown sugar

1 tsp of white vinegar, apple cider vinegar or balsamic vinegar

2 pods of crushed garlic

1 tbsp of finely chopped spring onion

1 tbsp each of finely chopped fresh herbs like basil, oregano, rosemary, etc.

Add the dressing to your chilled salad and toss well. To begin with, add a little bit of it at a time and keep tossing. Make sure that the dressing does not overwhelm the salad by making it slick, neither should it be so stingily put that you hardly get a taste. Everything should be lightly coated. Serve immediately with some toasted whole wheat bread and garlic butter.

Once you have the basics of a salad, feel free to mix and match different coloured leaves, fruits, veggies and cheeses according to your taste. Always steam the veggies before adding them to the salad. I rarely make the same salad twice.

Tomato Basil Bruschetta

Bruschetta is just a fancy name for an open sandwich.

This simple snack can be put together in a few minutes when hunger is nagging you or you don't have the time to whip up anything complicated.

Gather:
2 slices of bread
5 medium-sized tomatoes
A few glugs of olive oil
5 fresh basil leaves, roughly torn
Salt and pepper
1 tbsp of any cheese you fancy

Toast the bread.

While it's toasting, peel and chop the tomatoes into small pieces. Transfer to a bowl. Add the basil leaves.

Drizzle olive oil generously on the chopped tomatoes. Add a generous tbsp (or more, depending on how cheesy you want it) of crumbled or grated cheese of any kind – I like to use smoked gouda, ricotta or feta. Plain old Amul cheese works great as well.

Add a dash of salt and pepper to taste.

Mix everything well.

Put the toasted bread on a plate and lavishly pile on the tomato mixture. Eat at once!

You may leave out the cheese if you wish or add anything else to the tomato mixture that you like. Gently sautéed mushrooms, finely chopped bell peppers, baby corn, jalapenos, etc., all taste fantastic on a bruschetta. Experiment and come up with your own recipes for this really versatile snack.

Green Chutney

Gather:
(For the chutney)
½ coconut, desiccated
A huge bunch of coriander, washed and roughly chopped
1 inch piece of ginger, grated
3 pods of garlic, squashed and finely chopped
Juice of one lemon, freshly squeezed
4 green chillies
2 tbsps of organic brown sugar
Salt to taste
Optionally a 1tbsp of curd
(For the seasoning or tadka)
1 tsp mustard seeds (rai)
2 tsps cumin seeds (jeera)
1 green chilli, split
1 tsp ghee

Add all the chutney ingredients to a mixie and blend till thick and smooth. You may add a wee bit of curd if it's not blending, just to provide some moisture.

Empty the chutney into a bowl.

Heat a tbsp. of ghee in a small pan, add mustard seeds and cumin seeds and let them splutter for a few seconds. Add a split green chilli and cook it for less than a minute. Gently stir this seasoning (tadka) into the green chutney.

Butter a toasted slice of bread and spread this chutney on it. It's fabulous just like this.

Butter a slice of bread, spread a generous amount of the chutney. Add a few slices of tomato and a slice of any cheddar (Amul) cheese. Cover with another slice of buttered bread and grill for a truly divine Tomato Chutney Cheese Toasty.

This chutney is perfect with pakodas, samosas, batatavadas and other fried Indian savouries. A friend of mine eats it with plain rice and ghee!

Chatpat Paneer

250 gm paneer
Oil for sautéing or baking
Chat masala
Salt and pepper to taste
Fresh coriander leaves for garnish

Cut the paneer into medium-sized chunks. Spray with very little oil and bake at 200°C for five to seven minutes, till just cooked – a very light golden brown. It should remain soft inside and have just a tad of texture on the outside. It should not become chewy, which will happen if you leave it in too long. It's better if the paneer is undercooked rather than overcooked.

Alternatively, if you don't have an oven, sauté the paneer in a heavy-bottomed flat pan on medium heat.

Transfer to a plate. Add a few pinches of chat masala and a dash of salt and pepper. Garnish with finely chopped fresh coriander. Eat hot. Tastes great with green chutney.

The Generic Indian Subji

Wash and prep around 300 gm of your choice of vegetable or combination of veggies you want to cook. Potatoes take a while to cook, so it might be a good idea to boil them beforehand.

Heat 2 tbsps of oil or ghee in a heavy-bottomed vessel.

To create a basic seasoning for the veggies, add to the oil or ghee:

2 slit green chillies or 3 dried red chillies (more if you want it spicier)
1 tsp mustard seeds (rai)
2 tsps cumin seeds (jeera)
7-8 fresh curry leaves

For a more elaborate seasoning, you may add in some of the following:

2 tsps kitchen king powder
2 tsps dhania jeera powder
1 tsp red chilli powder
1 tsp turmeric powder
2 tsps tandoori chicken masala
2 tsps fish masala
2 tsps meat masala

Add in your veggies. Cover and cook on medium to low heat until the veggies are tender. Add salt and pepper to taste. To make the same veggies with gravy, simply peel and puree five medium-sized tomatoes and add this after your veggies are cooked. Simmer till the tomato paste is done, around fifteen minutes. Serve hot with any type of bread or roti.

In case anyone is wondering, the chicken, meat and fish masalas are all vegetarian and can be used to give a superb non-veggy twist to a completely vegetarian meal.

Rice

Gather:
1 fistful of rice for each person who will eat
1 tsp of ghee for each fistful of rice
Salt to taste

Wash the rice three or four times, totally draining the water each time. Put the rice in a pressure cooker and add water so that the water is about half an inch above the rice. If you add too much water, the rice will become sticky, if you add too less, it might burn. Once you make rice a few times, you will know exactly how much water to use.

Add in the ghee and the salt.

Pressure cook on high heat till you hear three whistles. Reduce heat to low and continue to cook for another ten minutes. Remove the cooker from the heat and let it stand and cool completely before opening it.

This method works for most types of white rice. However, polished white rice is quite unhealthy and I would recommend some type of unpolished rice or red rice. For this type of rice, after washing, soak the rice for a few hours in warm water. You will need double the amount of water you would use for white rice. Pressure cook for five whistles and simmer for around twenty minutes.

It's best not to reheat the rice and eat it steaming hot as soon as it is cooked.

This plain rice tastes great with all types of dals, rasam, sambhar, etc.

There is a very quick way to transform this plain rice into a yummy pulao.

For four fistfuls of rice,
Gather:
5 tomatoes, peeled and cut into chunks
2 big potatoes cut into bite-sized chunks (don't peel the potatoes)
A handful of green peas
A few cauliflower and/or broccoli florets.
2 carrots, cut into chunks
2 dried red chillies
1 two-inch cinnamon stick
5 cardamoms, split
5 cloves
1 tbsp garam masala
1 tbsp dhania-jeera powder
1 tbsp kitchen king powder
1 tsp turmeric powder

Heat oil in the pressure cooker. Put the red chillies, cinnamon, cardamoms and cloves in and let them cook for a minute. Add all the masalas and cook on low heat till fragrant.

Add all the veggies and stir to coat them with the spices.

Add in the rice and water. Pressure cook as usual. Voila! You got pulao!

If you have already made the plain rice, cook all the veggies and spices thoroughly and add to the plain rice. Mix everything up, taking care to do it gently so you don't break the rice.

If you skip all the masalas and the veggies and just add the cinnamon, cloves and cardamom to the pressure cooker, you will get very nice fragrant plain rice.

You can get creative with what veggies and what spices you add to the rice. Add mushrooms and bell peppers along with some hoisin sauce to get an oriental-flavoured pulao, for example. Have fun exploring!

Dal

There are many types of lentils or dals. We will concern ourselves with just two over here – the yellow moong dal and tuvar or arhar dal. The recipe below works for either one or a combination of both.

Gather:
One fistful of dal per person
1 tsp of ghee per fistful of dal, little more to make it richer
½ tsp turmeric powder per fistful of dal
Salt to taste

Wash and soak the dals in warm water for at least an hour, preferably overnight.

For a thick hearty dal, put it in a pressure cooker and add water so that the water is about one inch above the dal. Add more water for a thinner dal. Add the ghee, turmeric and salt. Pressure cook for three to five whistles and simmer for fifteen minutes after. Wait until the cooker has cooled before opening.

You may wish to blend the dal to make it silky smooth or leave it just like that. This is the most basic dal and it's great with plain rice.

A tadka will transform it from simple plain dal into something quite interesting.

Heat ghee and add two slit green chillies, a tsp of mustard seeds (rai) and two tsps of cumin (jeera) seeds. Cook till they splutter. Add in five curry leaves and cook till leaves are slightly wilted. Stir the entire mixture into your dal.

You can get creative with the tadka by adding some more spices like dhania or jeera, red chilli powder, kitchen king powder, etc.

You may also add one or more of the following:
Chunks of tomatoes
Chopped spinach
Drumstick leaves
to your dal to give it more flavour and texture. I normally add these to my tadka and cook them well before adding everything to the dal. Dal gets tastier the more it cooks and the more it stands. If you have the time, it's a great idea to simmer the dal for about thirty minutes. One-day-old, well-made dal can be quite a gastronomical experience!

Stewed Apples

This is a very simple dainty dessert that I first had at Prama and Ranji Bhandari's home in Delhi. It is a no-fuss preparation and gets done in no time. It's a fantastic light ending to a hearty meal and everyone who has had it till date loves it.

Gather:

2 apples

Peel and cut each apple into four quarters, then cut each quarter lengthwise into three pieces, so you will have twelve pieces from each apple.

2 two-inch sticks of cinnamon (dal chinni)

4 cloves (laung)

3 cardamoms, split (elaichi)

15 tbsps maple syrup or honey

The juice of one big lemon, freshly squeezed

Optional: Few scoops of whipped cream or few scoops of banana and/or vanilla ice cream

3 pinches cinnamon powder for garnish

In a medium-sized heavy-bottomed pan, bring to boil one and a half glasses of water. Add to this cinnamon sticks, cloves and cardamoms.

Put all the apple pieces into the boiling water, add a few pinches of cinnamon powder and cook for about twenty minutes, until the apples are very tender.

Add maple syrup or honey and the lemon juice. Adjust the honey/maple syrup and the lemon juice according to your taste of sweetness and tartness.

Serve in little bowls just like that, or with fresh whipped cream sprinkled with a pinch of cinnamon powder, or with a banana or vanilla ice cream.

The apples can be served either hot, room temperature or cold. I love them deliciously hot and tender, with a scoop of cold French vanilla ice cream.

Mango Cream Pie

This is a simple layered dessert. However, there is a lot of waiting involved because each layer has to be cooled and set before the next layer is added. There is not much effort involved, but considerable time will be required to put this together, so plan well in advance. You should start making this at least four hours before you intend to serve it.

Gather:
  1 small ripe pineapple, diced
  3 juicy ripe apples, washed and diced, don't bother peeling
  3-4 ripe Alphonso mangoes, pulped
  1 ripe Alphonso mango, thinly sliced for decoration
  3 packets of any biscuit that you like (We used Café Coffee Day's Honey Oatmeal, but something with ginger in it will be very nice too.)
  500 ml whipping cream.
  About 3-5 tbsps of melted butter
  1tbsp powdered organic sugar (optional)

Put the biscuit powder in a bowl and add the melted butter to it. Thoroughly blend in the butter.

Grease a baking tray with butter and add the buttered biscuit powder and press in firmly. Put this in the fridge to chill for at least thirty minutes.

Melt two tbsps of butter in a frying pan and add the apple and pineapple pieces and cook on low flame for about fifteen minutes until most of the moisture has evaporated and the fruit mixture is tender. You may optionally add a tbsp of powdered organic sugar. Let this cool for a bit. Remove the baking tray from the fridge and spread this (somewhat cooled) fruit mixture evenly on the biscuit base. Return the tray to the fridge for another half an hour.

Whip the cream till it forms soft peaks. Carefully stir five tbsps of the whipped cream into the mango pulp.

Bring out your tray from the fridge and carefully spread the mango cream on to the fruit layer. Make sure that the fruit layer is cold before doing this otherwise the cream will separate. Return the tray to the fridge for another half an hour.

Continue whipping the cream until it forms stiff peaks. With a spatula, spread a generous amount of the stiffly whipped cream onto the fruit and mango cream layers. If possible, do this step in a cool place. The cream layer should be little over slightly an inch thick. Smoothen out the cream layer with a spatula. Decorate with thinly sliced mangoes. Chill in the fridge for about an hour, more is better.

While serving, cut carefully into generous pieces and eat with relish...

PS: When mangoes are out of season, use (preferably) unsweetened mango pulp for making the mango cream. Or you could replace the mango cream layer with a jam layer. Add a teaspoon of butter to a frying pan and melt. Add ten tbsps of jam. I use an entire bottle of St Dalfours jam. After much experimenting, I have settled for one of mango and pineapple jam, apricot jam, strawberry jam or raspberry jam for this dessert. Cook the jam until it liquefies, you may need to add 1-4 tbsps of water. Then add this liquid jam to the fruit mixture instead of the mango cream layer. It tastes phenomenal!

Whipping Cream

Since whipped cream is a part of two of the recipes, I thought it would be nice to know how to make it. Just make sure you do the process in a cold kitchen.

Gather:
    250 gm packet whipping cream/double cream
    Ice cubes
    Bottle of cold water
    1 tbsp organic crystal sugar, powdered
    1 tbsp vanilla essence

Put the whipping cream in the fridge, not the freezer, so that it's very cold but not frozen. A few hours is enough. Don't use the Amul fresh cream that you get in the tetra pack. This method doesn't work with the Amul cream. You will need to ask for whipping cream or double cream from a good dairy or hypermarket.

You will need two bowls; a big bowl to make an ice bath for a second smaller bowl. Put both these in the freezer for a few hours, so they are very cold. The beater parts of your electric blender (don't even try this by hand) can be put in the freezer too to make very cold.

Once everything is cold, move fairly quickly.

In the big bowl, pour some of the cold water and a few ice cubes and place the smaller bowl in that ice bath. Add the cream to the smaller bowl till it's about one-third full.

Whip the cream with your beater until soft peaks form, then remove the beater.

Add the powdered sugar and a tbsp of vanilla essence. Whip again. Stop in about a minute if you want cream that forms soft peaks.

If you whip too long, the cream will separate and you will get butter, so be careful about that. Just before the cream becomes butter, it will get a very slight yellowish tinge. Stop whipping at this point.

Stiffly whipped cream will form firm peaks, and the blender will leave a trail in the cream.

Put the whipped cream into the fridge. It stays for some time; people say one week or so. (I don't know; every time I make whipped cream it gets over in about six minutes!)

Serve with the stewed apples or use in the mango cream pie.

If you don't add the sugar and vanilla essence, the same cream goes really well with savoury food. For example, combine some finely chopped fresh herbs like basil or chives with the cream and serve with baked potatoes.

THE SURYA NAMASKARS

1. Stand tall at the edge of your mat so that the rest of the mat is behind you, keep your feet together and balance your weight equally on both the feet. As you breathe in, expand your chest, lift both arms up from the sides and as you exhale, bring your palms together in front of the chest in prayer or namaste position. Press your hands together and push them a little downwards. Tighten the muscles of your whole arms and chest.

2. Breathing in, lift the arms up and back, keeping the biceps close to the ears. In this pose, the effort is to stretch the whole body up, from the heels to the tips of the fingers. You may push the pelvis forward a little bit. Ensure you're reaching up with the fingers rather than trying to bend backwards.

3. Breathing out, bend forward from the waist, keeping the spine erect. As you exhale completely, bring the hands down to the floor, curling the spine slowly, one vertebra at a time, beside the feet.

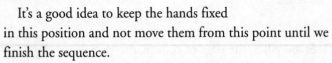

You may bend the knees, if necessary, to bring the palms down to the floor and then make a gentle effort to straighten the knees.

It's a good idea to keep the hands fixed in this position and not move them from this point until we finish the sequence.

4. Breathing in, push your right leg back, as far back as possible. Bring the right knee to the floor, push the lower back down and raise your head up, as if looking at the Sun, and smile.

5. As you breathe in, take the left leg back and bring the whole body in a straight line like a plank at an angle.

6. Gently bring your knees down to the floor and exhale. Take the hips back slightly, slide forward, rest your chest and chin on the floor.

Raise your buttocks up a little bit.

The two hands, two feet, two knees, chest and chin (eight parts of the body) touch the floor.

7. Slide forward and raise the chest up into the cobra posture. You may keep your elbows bent in this pose, the shoulders away from the ears. Raise your head to look up.

As you inhale, make a gentle effort to push the chest forward; as you exhale, make a gentle effort to push the body into the ground and especially the navel downwards. Ensure you're stretching just as much as you can; do not force.

8. Breathing out, lift the hips and the tailbone up, chest downwards in an 'inverted V' (/\) posture.

Keep the heels on the ground and make a gentle effort to lift the tailbone up, going deeper into the stretch.

9. Breathing in, bring the right foot forward in between the two hands, left knee down to the floor, press the hips down and raise your head, as if looking up to the Sun, and smile.

10. Breathing out, bring the left foot forward. Keep the palms on the floor. You may bend the knees, if necessary. Gently straighten the knees and if you can, try and touch your nose to the knees. With every deep breath, go more and more into the stretch and relax.

11. Breathing in, slowly roll the spine up, hands go up and bend backwards a little bit, pushing the hips slightly outward.

12. As you exhale, first straighten the body, then bring the arms together in the namaste pose. Push the palms against each other and downwards.

   Through position four to nine keep your glutes and thighs tight for maximum benefit.

   In other positions keep your stomach braced and tucked in to exercise the abdominals.

   When done with awareness of the muscles and organs, the surya namaskars become a fabulous physical exercise. When done with chanting and awareness of the breath and the chakras (nerve-plexes and emotions centres), the surya namaskars become a spiritual practice.

THE EXERCISES

Super Brain Yoga

Stand with your feet shoulder wide apart. Square your shoulders, chest up.

With your left hand hold your right earlobe. Cross your right hand over your left hand and hold the right ear lobe. Pull the ears slightly.

Make sure you are looking straight ahead and squat down with your spine erect.

As you go down take your butt back so that your knees do not cross the line of the toes and the butt goes below the knees. Then come up and straighten to the starting position.

Make sure you breathe in as you go down and breathe out as you come back up.

Do twenty-one squats.

Curl your fingers over your thumb to form a fist. Gently tap just above your temples with your fists a few times remembering the elephant-headed God – Ganesha.

Develops the capabilities of the brain, strengthens lower back, thighs and glutes, good for the liver and stomach.

Plank

Lie down on your stomach.

Keeping your arms from the elbows to the palms on the floor and the toes on the floor, balance your body in straight line like a plank.

Make sure the hips are not up or down but in a straight line with the back and the legs.

Tighten the thighs and glutes, pull the stomach in and brace the shoulders and arms.

Breathe with the whole body.

Incoming breath strengthens, outgoing breath relaxes.

Start with holding this pose for twenty seconds and over time build up to one minute. It's fantastic if you can hold it for three minutes.

Great for the core, arms and shoulders.

V Crunches

Lie down on your back.

Straighten your legs keeping them together and keep your arms straight above your head. Keeping both the arms and legs straight, slowly raise them.

Breathe out as you reach out with the arms at the top to touch the toes and crunch your tummy.

Breathe in as you slowly come back to starting position.

Make sure you don't let the legs and arms touch the floor between reps.

Do ten reps.

Variation: Breathe out as you bend the legs at the knees and pull the thighs close to the chest. Let the arms come up and touch the toes. Breathe in and straighten the legs and take the arms back above the head. Legs and arms don't touch the floor between reps.

Do ten reps.

Mainly for the stomach and abs.

Push-ups

Lie down on your stomach.

Keep your palms on the floor in front of your chest, hands straight, toes on the floor and body in a straight line parallel to the ground.

As you inhale, lower your torso so that your chest almost touches the floor, keeping the body straight.

Breathe out and use your hands to push your body up into the plank position, keeping your toes on the floor.

Exhale and push your body up, back into the starting position.

Do as many reps as possible.

To make it easier, you can rest your knees on the floor while doing push-ups.

To make it tougher you can put your toes on a higher surface.

Fantastic for the chest, shoulders and arms.

Hindu Push-up

If push-ups are too easy for you, try these. While push-ups work out the chest, shoulders, triceps and biceps, these give more of a full body workout and are much tougher to do than simple push-ups.

Keep your palms on the floor, toes on the floor, with your feet a little wider than your shoulders and the body in a straight line.

Without bending your knees, touch your heels to the floor and move your body to get the butt up in the air. Breathe in as you do this.

In a fluid motion, as you breathe out, bend your elbows so that your body comes forward and hips go down towards the floor and you end up in the cobra pose.

Tighten the lower back and abs.

As much as possible, while breathing in, retrace your movements and come back to starting position.

Even a few reps of these is a fabulous, almost full body workout.

Lunges with Swinging Arms

Keep your legs wide apart, twice your shoulder width.

Turn your head, your torso from the hip upwards and the corresponding foot to one side and bend that knee down till the thigh is parallel to the ground and the knee is not beyond the toe simultaneously swing the arms straight up. Breathe in as you do this.

While breathing out, simultaneously lower the arms as you straighten the legs.

Do ten reps.

Repeat on the other side.

Superb for glutes and thighs, works on the trapezius muscles of the shoulders as well.

Calf and Forearm Bounce

I

Stand with your feet a foot apart.

Turn your toes inwards so that the heels are far apart.

Straighten your hands above your head with the palms open downwards, bent perpendicular at the wrist, fingers outstretched, pointing inwards.

Raise yourself on the toes and clench the fists. Feel the tightness in your forearms and calves. Open and close the fists as you bounce your body up and down on the toes around twenty times.

II

Stand with your feet a foot apart.

Turn your toes outwards so that the heels are close together.

Straighten your hands above your head with the palms open downwards, bent perpendicular at the wrist, fingers outstretched, pointing outwards.

Raise yourself on the toes and clench the fists. Feel the tightness in your forearms and calves. Open and close the fists as you bounce your body up and down on the toes around twenty times.

III

Stand with your feet a foot apart. Your toes point forward.

Straighten your hands above your head and keep the palms open upwards, fingers outstretched, pointing backwards.

Raise yourself on the toes and clench the fists. Feel the tightness in your forearms and calves. Open and close the fists as you bounce your body up and down on the toes around twenty times.

To make this exercise easier, you can do the leg bounce separately from the hand squeezing.

Twists and Swings

Stand with feet shoulder width apart. Twist your upper body to the right from the hip, keeping the legs firmly on the ground, swinging both the arms above the shoulder level and look to the back on the right. The right arm will be raised above the shoulder, the left should touch the right shoulder.

Twist all the way to the left, mirroring the first swing – you are swinging both the arms above the shoulder level and looking to the back on the left. The left arm will be raised above the shoulder, the right should touch the left shoulder.

Do ten reps.

Continue with the twists, bringing the arms down a little, so that now both the arms are at shoulder level while you continue to look towards the back at the extreme position of each swing.

Do ten reps.

Finally, while you continue with the twists, bring both your arms to the level of your hips and look towards the back at the extreme position of the twist.

Do ten reps.

Breathe out when you are at the extreme positions for all three swings.

Strengthens, loosens up and brings flexibility to the entire spine.

Bird Bounce

Keep your feet firmly on the ground, little more than shoulder width apart, toes pointing outwards.

Take your arms up from the sides, like the wings of a bird. Touch the back of your palms to each other above your head.

Bring them down and bring the palms together in front of your crotch as your bend your knees.

Take your arms back up above your head and touch the back of your palms to each other as you straighten your legs.

As you come back down, this time touch your palms to each other behind your butt.

Breathe in as your hands go up, breathe out as your hands come down.

Alternate like this for ten reps.

Brilliant for inner thighs and hips and great for the shoulders.

FOCUSING TECHNIQUES

The two techniques given below are fabulous for increasing your focus and concentration levels for a few hours.

Do them just before you start your work, you will be amazed by how little your mind wanders and how much you manage to get done.

As with any technique, the more you practise, the better will be the result.

Nadi Shodhan Pranayam

Sit comfortably with your spine erect. Close your eyes.

Rest your left hand on your left thigh in chin mudra – tip of the index finger lightly touching the thumb and the rest of the fingers gently outstretched together.

Gently touch the index and middle finger of the right hand inbetween the eyebrows.

With your thumb, gently close your right nostril and breathe out from the left nostril.

Begin round one:

Breathe in through the left nostril. After you finish breathing in, with your middle finger and ring finger, gently close your left nostril, simultaneously lifting your thumb from the right nostril. Breathe out from the right nostril.

Breathe in from the right nostril; then, gently close it with the thumb while simultaneously opening the left nostril by lifting the ring and little fingers. Breathe out from the left.

This completes round one. Do at least nine more rounds.

Tratak

Sit comfortably with the spine erect.

Stretch your right arm straight in front of your face, with your thumb up and four fingers in a light fist.

Look at the fingernail of the thumb.

Keeping your gaze on the fingernail of your thumb, raise your arm up slowly, till the point you can't see it. Then bring it down slowly into your lap. Then bring it up to the eye level and take it to the right to the side of the body, till the point you can't see it. Bring it back to the centre.

Repeat the process similarly with the left hand – up, down and to the left.

Then with the right hand, still with thumb up and light fist, make full circle at the edge of your vision while keeping sight on the thumbnail so that your eyeballs roll clockwise. Repeat anticlockwise.

Repeat the above with the left hand, clockwise and anti clockwise.

Finally, bring the thumb back to the starting position, right in front of the face. Slowly bend your arm to bring the thumb to the tip of your nose. Slowly stretch your arm back out to the starting position.

With the arm outstretched, look beyond the tip of the thumb to the wall or to infinity and then return your gaze back to the thumb.

Relax both hands.

Blink your eyes a few times. Every time you close them, squeeze tightly.

SRI SRI RAVI SHANKAR

Gurudev Sri Sri Ravi Shankar is a universally revered spiritual and humanitarian leader. His vision of a violence-free, stress-free society through the reawakening of human values has inspired millions to broaden their spheres of responsibility and work towards the betterment of the world.

He is a multi-faceted social visionary whose initiatives include conflict resolution, disaster and trauma relief, poverty alleviation, empowerment of women, prisoner rehabilitation, education for all and campaigns against female foeticide and child labour. He is engaged in peace negotiations and counselling in conflict zones around the world.

In 1981, he established the Art of Living, an educational and humanitarian non-governmental organization. In 1997, Gurudev founded the International Association for Human Values (IAHV) to foster human values and lead sustainable development projects. He is also a co-founder of India Against Corruption (IAC).

He has reached out to many millions of people worldwide through personal interactions, public events, teachings, Art of Living workshops and humanitarian initiatives. He has brought to the masses ancient practices that were traditionally kept exclusive and has designed many self-development techniques that can easily be integrated into daily life to calm the mind and instil confidence and enthusiasm. One of Gurudev's most unique offerings to the world is the Sudarshan Kriya, a powerful breathing technique that facilitates physical, mental, emotional and social well-being.

Numerous honours have been bestowed upon him, including the highest civilian awards of Colombia, Mongolia and Paraguay. In 2016, he was conferred with the Padma Vibhushan, one of the highest civilian awards of India. Gurudev has addressed several international forums, including TED 2010 at Monterey, the United Nations Millennium World Peace Summit (2000), the World Economic Forum (2001, 2003) and several parliaments across the globe.

Gurudev travels to nearly 40 countries every year, exemplifying his call to globalize wisdom.

His universal and simple message is that love and wisdom can prevail over hatred and distress.

THE ART OF LIVING COURSES

THE ART OF LIVING

Sri Sri Ravi Shankar created the Art of Living Foundation (as Ved Vignan Mahavidyapeeth) in 1981. It offers many self-development courses for individuals and communities.

It's a well-established scientific fact that happy people are more productive, creative, efficient and effective. Who wouldn't want all this and more in their lives? Gift yourself this 'happiness advantage' by engaging yourself with Art of Living's various programmes.

And if you are thinking – But I am already happy ... surely you are not allergic to more happiness?!

The Happiness Programme

Weight gain (or loss) without a diet change, hairfall, stomach ache and stomach disorders, forgetfulness, sleep disorders, headaches, frequent colds and infections are just a few symptoms of stress.

Most people just accept stress and tension as part of their lives. They feel that they simply have to 'cope' with the problems associated with stress and get on with life.

The Art of Living Happiness Programme has many techniques that allow you to de-stress and live your life without all the associated distress!

There is whole new field called positive psychology. It's founded on the belief that people want to lead meaningful and fulfilling lives, to cultivate what is best within themselves and to enhance their experiences of love, work and play. In the Art of Living courses, the yoga, meditation techniques and interactive processes that you will experience release all the right hormones in your system, which allows you to do exactly that.

The profound and powerful Sudarshan Kriya that is taught in the programme enables you to effortlessly let go of your stresses and tensions and introduces within you a tranquillity you never knew existed. So you can be what you always wanted to be – healthy, poised, calm, relaxed and confident.

The YES!+ Programme

A person who is twelve or thirteen can't wait to be eighteen. A thirty-five to forty-year-old, yearns for his youth. Everyone wants to be eighteen … except the ones who *are* eighteen!

The age from eighteen to thirty is a wonderful time in life. You feel you can do absolutely anything. That you can conquer the world! Your body and mind are at their peak. Unfortunately, so is the confusion. There are so many options. There are so many challenges. To top it off, you have raging hormones. Things you do or don't in this time can profoundly affect the rest of your life.

You desperately need a calm, poised mind to be able to take sensible decisions. The YES!⁺ course was created by Dinesh and I under the guidance of Sri Sri Ravi Shankar to address all these issues and more.

Sparkling with dialogue, peppered with fun and humour, liberally sprinkled with insightful interactive processes, all enveloped with exploring a dimension of the mind most people don't even know exist, this course is a delectable treat for a young person who wants to go places.

The Sudarshan Kriya is taught within this course, along with a few techniques to enhance focus and concentration levels.

You will have the tools and the ability to be able to live the life you *want* to live, instead of the life you *have* to live.

The Advanced Meditation Course

The AMC is a residential four to ten day silence programme. It begins early in the morning with yoga and Sudarshan Kriya, has guided meditation sessions through the day and ends with blissful chanting and knowledge from Sri Sri in the evening. Tasty, healthy food is served to all course participants at meal times.

It helps you recharge and rejuvenate yourself so that you are better equipped to deal with the stresses and challenges that contemporary life throws at you with equanimity and poise. It is a super intensive workout for the mind and body and people who have undergone this course come out feeling utterly refreshed, their faces aglow and their hearts at peace.

After more than two decades of practising meditation, Dinesh and I still do one AMC every year, and we recommend that you do, too. Take a few days off, unplug yourself from the world and totally relax.

Though AMCs are now conducted in cities and towns all over the world, we feel the best way to get the most out of them is to go do them at one of Art of Living's many ashrams.

Our favourite places to do an AMC? The Art of Living ashrams in Bangalore, Rishikesh, Gujarat, Germany, the US and Canada.

Sahaj Samadhi Meditation

Everyone has experienced a meditative state in moments of deep joy or when completely engrossed in an activity, when just for a few moments the mind becomes light and at ease. Almost all of us have sporadically experienced such moments of utter calm and peace, but we are unable to repeat them at will. The Sahaj Samadhi Meditation programme teaches you how. This technique almost instantly alleviates the practitioner from stress-related problems, deeply relaxes the mind and rejuvenates the system.

'Sahaj' is a Sanskrit word that means natural or effortless. 'Samadhi' is a deep, blissful, meditative state. 'Sahaj Samadhi Meditation' is a natural, effortless system of meditation.

Regular practise of the technique can totally transform the quality of one's life by culturing the system to maintain peace, energy and expanded awareness throughout the day.

There are many other courses that Art of Living offers, from learning yoga to vegetarian cooking and almost everything in between.

The teachers and volunteers of the Art of Living Foundation strive to create a better world for themselves and their communities through various service activities like planting trees, rejuvenating rivers, running free schools in villages and slums, empowering women, providing vocational training for village youth, helping disaster victims, etc. You will find descriptions and details of all this and more on our website www.artofliving.org.

FURTHER READING

1. *An Intimate Note to the Sincere Seeker* – **Sri Sri Ravi Shankar**

Little capsules of wisdom, hardly more than a page long, sometimes funny, sometimes mischievous and always profound. A wonderful read – you will have many, many 'a-ha!' moments.

2. *A Mind for Numbers* – **Barbara Oakley**

A brilliant book about how to study – especially maths and science. Barbara Oakley runs a lovely online course on Coursera called Learning to Learn. I came across the course as my book was going into print.

3. *The Happiness Track* – **Emma Seppälä**

Emma Seppälä explains that behind our inability to achieve sustainable fulfilment are counterproductive theories of success. Success doesn't have to come at our personal expense. Drawing on the latest research into resilience, will-power, growth mindset, stress, creativity, compassion, mindfulness, gratitude training and optimism, Emma shows how nurturing ourselves is the most productive thing we can do to thrive professionally and personally. Filled with practical advice on how to apply these findings to your daily life, *The Happiness Track* is a life-changing guide to fast-tracking your success and creating an anxiety-free life.

4.   *The Happiness Advantage* – Shawn Achor

Conventional wisdom holds that if we work hard we will be more successful, and if we are more successful, then we'll be happy. If we can just find that great job, win that next promotion, lose those five pounds, happiness will follow. But recent discoveries in the field of positive psychology have shown that this formula is actually backward: happiness fuels success, not the other way around. Shawn Achor explores this idea in this superbly written book.

5.   *A Journey through Genius* – William Dunham

A history of ten great theorems of mathematics. Stories and proofs of theorems abound. Presented with a sprinkling of humour, this is an intensely readable book for anyone who wants to know more about maths and mathematicians.

6.   *A Short History of Nearly Everything* – Bill Bryson

One of my absolute favourite books by Bill Bryson. This book is what every textbook wants to be when it grows up. Jam-packed with facts and stories written with his typical dry humour, the illustrated hard cover version of this book is a must read for everyone.

7. *Last Chance to See* – **Douglas Adams and Mark Carwardine**

'We put a big map of the world on a wall, Douglas stuck a pin in everywhere he fancied going, I stuck a pin in where all the endangered animals were, and we made a journey out of every place that had two pins.' A superb travelogue, an eye-opening look at the fragile beauty of the wild.

8. *Reality is Broken* – **Jane McGonigal**

Why play computer games? how playing games is *not* a waste of time as many see it to be but can be therapeutic and enhance productivity and creativity in all of us. If you are a gamer, read this one. If you are not, read it to see what turns us gamers on, and what you are missing out on!

9. *Food Revolution* – **John Robbins**

The best book according to me about how the meat-based diet a lot of people eat is ravaging our planet, bringing disease into our bodies, causing horrific suffering to innocent animals and costing governments billions upon billions of dollars. Written in a clean, clinical, non-emotional way, this is the best argument I know of for switching to a vegetarian diet. Please read.

10. *Indian Super Foods* – **Rujuta Divekar**

Forget all that firang food you find difficult to even pronounce, let alone eat. Our grandmothers were right all along. Rujuta writes with a pen dipped in sarcasm that I totally enjoy. She gets her point across brilliantly. Ghee is *really* good for you! Read and find out why.

11. *Gut: The Inside Story of Our Body's Most Underrated Organ* – Giulia Enders

This book is a cheeky, up-close and personal guide to the secrets and science of our digestive system. I thoroughly enjoyed it and was amazed at the goings on in my insides. There is a universe in there and it's at war! You get to decide who wins…

12. *The Tipping Point* – Malcolm Gladwell

How little things can make a big difference. I kind of always knew that, but I didn't know how little and how big. The tipping point is that magic moment when an idea, trend, or social behaviour crosses a threshold, tips and spreads like wildfire. Just as a single sick person can start an epidemic of the flu, so too can a small but precisely targeted push cause a fashion trend, the popularity of a new product or a drop in the crime rate. Malcolm Gladwell explores and brilliantly illuminates how the tipping point phenomenon is already changing the way people throughout the world think about selling products and disseminating ideas.

A superb must read book!

13. *The Secret Life of Stuff* – Julie Hill

Reduce and reuse instead of recycle. A thought-provoking informative book about what goes into making everyday stuff and where it all ends up when you throw it away.

14. *Rich Dad, Poor Dad* – Robert Kiyosaki

How do the super rich think? What do the super rich do? Could we do it too? Nice read, great ideas for growing wealth.

15. *Freakonomics* – **Steven D. Levitt and Stephen J. Dubner**
Can economics be interesting? Really?! Here is a book exploring the sex appeal, if you will, of economics. Below is an excerpt from their web page, talking more about the book.

'Which is more dangerous, a gun or a swimming pool? What do schoolteachers and sumo wrestlers have in common? Why do drug dealers still live with their moms? How much do parents really matter? How did the legalization of abortion affect the rate of violent crime?'

These may not sound like typical questions for an economist to ask. But Steven D. Levitt is not a typical economist. He is a much-heralded scholar who studies the riddles of everyday life – from cheating and crime to sports and child-rearing – and whose conclusions turn conventional wisdom on its head.

Freakonomics is a ground-breaking collaboration between Levitt and Stephen J. Dubner, an award-winning author and journalist. They usually begin with a mountain of data and a simple, unasked question. Some of these questions concern life-and-death issues; others have an admittedly freakish quality. Thus the new field of study contained in this book: Freakonomics.

16. *The Little Book That Beats the Market* – **Joel Greenblatt**
A superb starter book about the world of stocks and shares. Written in a way a completely lay person can understand, this book is invaluable if you are planning to invest in shares but don't know where to start. If there is going to be exactly one book you want to read on the share market, this should be the one!

17. *Pure and Simple* – Vidhu Mittal

This book has simple, easy-to-follow recipes with ingredients easily available in India. It is an outstanding cookbook for anyone interested in cooking vegetarian Indian khana at home.

18. *Blandings Castle* – P. G. Wodehouse

A list of 'books you should read' made by me can never be complete without having at least one book by P. G. Wodehouse. He has written over a hundred books, all about idyllic worlds full of sparkle, mischief, derring-do and happy endings. I have not read an author better than Wodehouse for exploring the sheer wonder the English language can make you feel while reading. He is a master at his craft, making his writing feel effortless and uproariously funny at the same time. *Blandings Castle* is my absolute favourite book by P. G. Wodehouse.